Essence Essay Writing

[일러두기]
이 책은 2012년 출간된 〈정통영어작문〉의 개정판입니다.

TOEIC · TOEFL · ESSAY
영어논술, 해외유학을 위한
영작문 바이블!

Essence
Essay
Writing

밴쿠버 SM Education 편저

Mindcube

머리글

*Essence Essay Writing*은 밴쿠버 성문학원(www.sungmoon.ca)의 교재입니다. 밴쿠버 성문학원은 캐나다 밴쿠버에 소재한 Writing 전문학원입니다. Oxford 대학 영문학박사 Dania Sheldon을 주축으로 한 성문개발팀이 다년간 연구개발한 Grammatical Writing, Pre-Essay, Essay Writing 등 3개 코스의 교재를 한국 실정에 맞게 정리한 것입니다.

이 책은 중급 및 고급 수준의 학생들을 대상으로 하며, TOEFL, TOEIC, SAT 등의 각종 시험, 영어논술, 그리고 해외 유학을 준비하는 학생들에게 많은 도움이 될 것입니다.

좋은 Writing을 하기 위해서는 어휘력, 문법, 글의 아이디어, 그리고 체계적이고 논리적으로 글쓰는 기법이 필요합니다. *Essence Essay Writing*은 글쓰는 기법을 공부하는 책입니다.

Writing을 집짓는 것에 비유하면 어휘력, 문법, 아이디어는 각각 자재, 도구, 설계도에 해당됩니다. 그리고 글쓰는 기법은 집 짓는 일에 비유할 수 있습니다. 실제로 캐나다에서 한국 학생들을 가르치다 보면, 가지고 있는 어휘력, 문법실력에 비해 Writing이 부족한 경우를 흔히 봅니다. 즉, 건축기술이 부족하여 가지고 있는 자재와 도구도 제대로 사용하지 못하고 집다운 집을 짓지 못하는 것입니다.

  *Essence Essay Writing*은 총 18개 Lesson으로 구성되어 있습니다. 그리고 각 Lesson마다 Writing Exercise를 두어 학생들이 Writing 연습을 하도록 하였습니다.

감사합니다.

밴쿠버 성문학원
원장 양성필

차례

Part I : Writing a Paragraph

Lesson 1: Structure of a Paragraph ··· 13
    1. What is a Paragraph? ··· 13
    2. Structure of a Paragraph ··· 13
    Writing Exercise ·· 21

Lesson 2: Narrowing the Topic and Writing a Topic Sentence ········· 25
    1. Narrowing the Topic ··· 25
    2. Topic and Controlling Idea ··· 27
    Writing Exercise ·· 32

Lesson 3: Body of a Paragraph ··· 37
    1. Creating Ideas ·· 37
    2. Selecting/ Dropping/ Arranging Ideas ··························· 39
    3. Paragraph Unity ·· 42
    Writing Exercise ·· 46

Lesson 4: Organizing a Paragraph ··· 51
    1. Time Order ··· 51
    2. Emphatic Order (Order of Importance) ························· 54
    3. Space Order ·· 56
    Writing Exercise ·· 58

Lesson 5: Paragraph Planning ·· 63
    1. Linear Diagramming ·· 63
    Writing Exercise 1 ··· 67
    2. Continuous Timed Writing ··· 68
    Writing Exercise 2 ··· 71

Lesson 6: Editing and Revising ··· 73
    1. Adding Ideas ··· 74
    2. Removing Unnecessary or Irrelevant Ideas ·· 78
    3. Rewording ·· 81
    4. Reordering ··· 85
    5. Proofreading ··· 86
    Writing Exercise ·· 87

Lesson 7: Effective Sentence Structure ··· 91
    1. Varying Sentence Structure ·· 91
    2. Sentence Combining ·· 98
    Writing Exercise ·· 107

Lesson 8: Use of Effective Language ·· 111
    1. Use of Descriptive Adjectives ··· 111
    2. Use of Descriptive Verbs ·· 116
    3. Use of Active and Passive Voice ·· 117
    4. Parallel Structure ··· 119
    Writing Exercise ·· 123

Part II : Writing an Essay

Lesson 9 : Structure of an Essay ··· 129
    1. Introductory Paragraph ··· 130
    2. Body Paragraphs ··· 131
    3. Conclusion ·· 132
    Writing Exercise ·· 139

Lesson 10: Developing a Thesis ·· 141
    1. What is a Thesis? ··· 141
    2. Limiting a Topic ·· 145
    3. Writing a Thesis Statement ·· 147
    4. Supporting the Thesis with Specific Ideas ·· 149
    Writing Exercise ·· 155

Lesson 11: Introduction and Conclusion ··· 157
    1. Writing an Introductory Paragraph ··· 157
    2. Six Ways of Writing an Introductory Paragraph ································· 158
    3. Three Ways of Writing a Concluding Paragraph ································ 162
    Writing Exercise ·· 165

Lesson 12: Connecting Ideas with Transitions ··· 167
    1. Transitions ·· 167
    2. Transitional Sentences ·· 171
    Writing Exercise ·· 177

Lesson 13: Persuasive/Argumentative Essay - Part 1 ································· 179
    1. What is Persuasion? ·· 179
    2. Methods of Persuasion ··· 180
    Writing Exercise ·· 187

Lesson 14: Persuasive/Argumentative Essay - Part 2 ································· 189
    1. Strategies for Argumentation ··· 189
    2. Indicating Awareness of the Opposing Opinion ····································· 194
    Writing Exercise ·· 199

Lesson 15: Cause and Effect Essay ··· 201
    1. Writing a Cause and Effect Paragraph ··· 202
    Writing Exercise – Paragraphs ··· 207
    2. Developing a Cause and Effect Essay ·· 210
    Writing Exercise ·· 214

Lesson 16: Definition Essay ·· 217
    1. Types of Definition ··· 218
    Writing Exercise ·· 225

Lesson 17: Division and Classification Essay ··· 227
    1. What is Classification? ··· 227
    2. Guidelines for Division/Classification Essay ··· 228
    Writing Exercise ·· 235

Lesson 18: Comparison and Contrast Essay ··· 237
    1. Contrast Paragraph ·· 238
    2. Comparison Paragraph ·· 242
    3. Comparison-Contrast Paragraph ··· 243
    4. Developing a Comparison or Contrast Essay ·· 246
    Writing Exercise ·· 252

Answer Keys ··· 255

Part I*

Writing a Paragraph

Lesson 1: Structure of a Paragraph

1. What is a Paragraph?

> Paragraph란 문단을 의미하며 일반적으로 6~12개의 문장으로 구성됩니다. Essay는 몇 개의 paragraph로 구성되며 (통상 5개), 좋은 essay를 쓰기위해서는 paragraph 작성기법을 숙지하는 것이 필수입니다.

A paragraph is a series of sentences which develop one single idea. There is no specifically designated length for a paragraph; however, most paragraphs that students are required to write are between six and twelve sentences long.

Sometimes you will be asked to write a paragraph to answer a question for homework, or on a test. However, the most frequent use of a paragraph is in an essay, which is actually a series of paragraphs based around one subject. But before you attempt to write longer pieces, it is important to be able to write a strong, clear, coherent, unified single paragraph.

2. Structure of a Paragraph

> Paragraph는 main idea (글의 주제), topic sentence (주제를 표현한 문장), body (주제를 뒷받침하는 세부사항) 그리고 concluding sentence (끝맺는 문장)으로 구성됩니다.

A paragraph consists of the **main idea**, the **topic sentence**, the **body** and the **concluding sentence**.

2-1. Main Idea and Topic Sentence

> 각 Paragraph에는 하나의 main idea가 있습니다. 또한 paragraph에 있는 모든 문장들은 그 main idea에 관한 것이어야만 합니다. Main idea를 표현한 문장이 topic sentence입니다. Topic sentence는 대부분의 경우에 paragraph의 맨처음에 위치합니다. 아래의 paragraph에서 topic sentence를 찾아봅시다.

A paragraph must contain only **one main idea**. Every sentence in the paragraph must relate to the one main idea.

The main idea is stated by the **topic sentence**. It will tell the reader the subject or **topic** of the paragraph. Most frequently, the topic sentence will be the first sentence in the paragraph. It is also possible to find the topic sentence of a paragraph in different locations in the paragraph.

Look at the following example:

> Winter is my favorite time of year. When the snow begins to fall, I feel a new energy and excitement. Soon I will be able to ski and snowboard on the mountains. There is nothing more beautiful than a day on the slopes with the wind in my face and the sound of the snow beneath my boards. When I am not skiing, I am skating on the pond on my neighbor's farm. There is always a group of enthusiastic hockey players ready for a game. One of the best times of the winter is when we go for a weekend trip on our snow machines. We follow the ready made paths up into the mountains, and there, when the snow is good, we blaze new trails through the forests and valleys. I am always sad to see the end of winter!

The **topic sentence** of this paragraph is: *Winter is my favorite time of year.*

All the other sentences tell the reader something about why the writer loves the winter.

2-2. Body

> Body 부분은 topic sentence를 뒷받침하고 설명하는 세부사항들을 포함합니다. 위의 paragraph에서는 4개의 예를 들어 winter를 좋아하는 이유를 설명했습니다.

The body of a paragraph tells the reader more about the topic sentence by using a number of methods to make the ideas clear.

Look back at the paragraph on Winter. The writer tells the reader all the reasons that he loves the winter. He gives the reader **examples** of the things that he likes. Look at the following organization of the paragraph:

Topic sentence: *Winter is my favorite time of year.*
Examples in the body of the paragraph (supporting points):
- skiing
- snowboarding
- skating/hockey
- snow machine riding

The body of this paragraph has eight sentences. It has taken the writer eight sentences to explain his topic sentence. He has used four supporting points to prove his topic sentence.

2-3. Concluding Sentence

> Concluding sentence는 paragraph를 끝맺는 문장으로 보통 1-2 문장으로 이루어집니다. 그러나 모든 paragraph에 concluding sentence가 필요하지는 않습니다. (특히 짧은 paragraph의 경우)

The conclusion of a paragraph summarizes or comments on the main idea in one or two sentences.

The concluding sentence for a stand-alone paragraph should accomplish one of the following:

- Restate the topic sentence of the paragraph
- Summarize by referring to the key points in the paragraph
- Draw a conclusion based on the information set forth in the paragraph
- Offer a final observation about the controlling idea
- Make a prediction based on the details of the paragraph

Often, the concluding sentences close the paragraph by returning to the main idea of the paragraph. They do this by repeating a key word or phrase from the topic sentence.

Topic Sentence:
   Parents can help their children be successful in school by encouraging them.

Concluding Sentence:
   So, if parents really want their children to succeed in school, they need to pay attention to their children's studies and encourage them.

Sometimes in the concluding sentences, the writer does not use the exact key words from the topic sentence but rephrases them, using other words that mean the same thing. This gives some variety to the paragraph. Notice how the key words in the topic sentence above could be rephrased:

Concluding Sentence:
   Parents who want their children to do their best in school must support and pay attention to them.

In this concluding sentence, do their best means the same as *succeed* and *support* means the same as *encourage*.

Not all academic paragraphs contain concluding sentences, especially if the paragraph is very short. However, if your paragraph is long, it is a good idea to use a concluding sentence.

A Note on Formality

In addition to having a particular kind of structure, academic paragraphs (and multi-paragraph essays) are different from "ordinary writing" (such as letter writing) in that certain kinds of expressions are not allowed. For example, in formal essays, you should not use contractions such as *don't* or *aren't*. Instead, you should write out the words in full, for example, *do not* and *are not*.

Also, in formal essays you should avoid the first and second person. That is, do **not** use the pronouns *I* or *you* except for certain types of writings such as Narrative Paragraphs/Essays. It is safer simply to use the third person.

Exercise 1

연습문제를 통해 paragraph의 topic sentence와 supporting points를 찾아봅니다.

For each of the following paragraphs:

    a. State the topic sentence
    b. List the supporting points used to support the topic sentence

1)   People should not drink and drive. Statistics have shown that 50% of all traffic accidents are alcohol related. Alcohol reduces a person's reaction time, so an accident could often have been avoided if the driver had not been drinking. As well, drunken drivers often fall asleep at the wheel, and lose control of their vehicles. Finally, a drunken driver may not be able to see clearly, and objects around him on the road may be blurred. As a result, the driver may not see the obstacles, that is, other vehicles or people on the road, and be unable to avoid them. Mixing alcohol and driving is simply not worth the risk.

a. Underline the topic sentence.

b. The supporting points are:

    i.

    ii.

    iii.

    iv.

2) Parents who read to their children on a regular basis are doing their children a great favor. Studies have shown that children who are exposed to reading early in life develop a love of reading that never leaves them. As well, they are better readers themselves than children who are not read to as infants. In addition, children who are read to are better writers. Statistics testing children of all ages show an incredible difference in the writing skills of children who are readers and those who are not. Reading to a child develops his sense of language and this development is a strong component in a child's success in school.

a. Underline the topic sentence.

b. The supporting points are:

    i.

    ii.

    iii.

    iv.

3) When I chose my university, my major consideration was location. I wanted to be close to home since I really could not afford to live in residence or in an apartment. But there were other considerations too. I wanted to be sure that the university had a strong academic environment in my field. As well, I wanted to have a place that gave

me options for my leisure. I hoped to find a university with a good ski team that I could join. For me, athletics is an important way to stay healthy and to get away from the books for a while. Finally, I wanted to find a university that was highly regarded by potential employers. There are certainly a lot of things to consider when choosing the best university to attend!

  a. Underline the topic sentence.

  b. The supporting points are:

    i.

    ii.

    iii.

    iv.

 Exercise 2

> 아래 각 문제에는 하나의 topic sentence와 세 개의 supporting points가 있습니다. 그 중 topic sentence를 골라보세요.

Each of the following groups of sentences contains one topic sentence and three supporting points. Choose the sentence that states the main idea and would serve as the topic sentence for each group.

Example:
  a. People often take Echinacea(에키나시아, 꽃의 일종) because they believe it will cure a cold.
  b. Garlic is said to be good for the bloodstream and for digestion.
  c. Natural herbs are being widely used to improve health.
  d. Ginseng is considered to be a stimulant for the central nervous system.

Topic Sentence: Natural herbs are being widely used to improve health.

This sentence includes all the ideas in the other sentences. The other supporting sentences give examples of this statement.

1) a. The sounds of playing children fill the sunny days.
    b. The power boats pull water-skiers from dawn till dusk.

    c. Tourists in their houseboats are as thick as flies on the water.
    d. Each summer, our lake is filled with activity.

Topic Sentence:

2) a. Learning to be financially accountable is most important.
    b. Getting and keeping a job is one of the first major steps.
    c. Being independent means learning to live responsibly.
    d. It is very important to learn to make sound decisions for yourself.

Topic Sentence:

3) a. Wild animals are often used to perform in circuses.
    b. Many animals are captured and placed into small cages in zoos.
    c. Human beings do not always treat animals with respect.
    d. Small animals which have been abandoned are often used in medical experiments.

Topic Sentence:

Exercise 3

> 아래 문제에 주어진 supporting point들에 대해 topic sentence를 만들어 보세요.

This exercise will test your ability to recognize the common theme of a group of ideas. We have given you the supporting points that would be used in a paragraph, and we want you to write the best topic sentence you can think of to unite the groups of points.

Look at this example:
    a. *The sounds of sirens often keep city dwellers awake at night.*
    b. *Agitated drivers blow their horns constantly.*
    c. *Noisy crowds line the streets day and night.*
    Topic Sentence: City life is noisy.
    All the supporting points describe the sounds of the city, so the topic sentence needs to reflect the noise.

Here are two for you to do. Write your topic sentence in the blank provided.

1) Topic Sentence:_____

   a. The flu shot (감기예방주사) is available for everyone and can help prevent illness.
   b. Babies and young children can get vaccinations for mumps(이하선염) and measles(홍역).
   c. Older people can get injections which contain important vitamins that they need for their health.

2) Topic Sentence:_____

   a. Cats do not have to be taken for a walk twice a day.
   b. Cats do not bark at people when they come to the door.
   c. Cats don't chew slippers and shoes.
   d. Cats can be left on their own for a day or two.

✏️ Writing Exercise

> 이번 lesson에서 배운 것을 사용하여 아래 topic으로 3개의 paragraph writing을 합니다. 다음 장에 있는 Paragraph Planning Sheet를 작성한 후 writing을 하세요.

Choose **three** topics, and then write **three** paragraphs. Complete the planning sheets in the next pages. Each paragraph must be 125-150 words in length.

Here are the topic sentences to choose from:

1) My bedroom is the messiest room in our house.

2) I don't know how I would get along without my best friend.

3) There are several ways to make money when you are a teenager.

4) I really love (hate) to go camping/vacation in the summer.

5) I really love (hate) to go skiing/snowboarding in the winter.

6) Parents should (should not) spank children who are misbehaving.

7) People judge others by the clothes they wear.

8) Money does not buy happiness.

Paragraph Planning Sheet

Topic Sentence:

Ideas to support the topic sentence:

1.

2.

3.

Concluding Idea

Paragraph Planning Sheet

Topic Sentence:

Ideas to support the topic sentence:

1.

2.

3.

Concluding Idea

Paragraph Planning Sheet

Topic Sentence:

Ideas to support the topic sentence:

1.

2.

3.

Concluding Idea

Lesson 2: Narrowing the Topic and Writing a Topic Sentence

1. Narrowing the Topic

> Topic이 주어진 후 글을 쓰기 위한 첫단계가 "Narrowing the Topic (Topic의 범위 좁히기)"입니다. Topic은 넓은 범위를 포함합니다. Topic의 범위를 좁혀 하나의 paragraph에 포함될 수 있는 주제를 선정하는 과정을 "Narrowing the Topic"이라고 합니다. 아래의 예는 "my bedroom"이라는 topic에서 narrowing된 여러 topic sentence들을 보여줍니다.

A writer must go through a series of steps to design a good paragraph. The first step is to **narrow** the topic.

When you are writing a paragraph for school or a test, you will probably be given only a **topic** and you will have to write your own **topic sentence**.

For example:
Your teacher might ask you to write a paragraph describing your bedroom.
The topic is: *My Bedroom*
But your **topic sentence** might be: *My bedroom is the messiest room in our house.*

The topic sentence is actually a sentence, but the topic may be expressed in one or two words. So, how do you get from the topic to the topic sentence?

As you can see from the example above, the topic that was given is very broad. There are a lot of things that could be said about your bedroom. Look at some of the following possibilities:

My bedroom is well organized
My bedroom is beautifully decorated
My bedroom is filled with special things
My bedroom is messy
My bedroom is a quiet place

You have a number of choices here. Since you cannot describe everything about the room in one paragraph, you have to choose what you want to say about the bedroom.

This process is called **narrowing the topic**. When you narrow the topic, you make it small enough to deal with in one paragraph.

In lesson 1, you were given the topic sentence "My bedroom is the messiest room in the house". So the writer would talk only about the messy things in the bedroom and none of the other aspects of it. If the writer also wanted to talk about the 'special things' in the bedroom, then he would have to write another paragraph with a new topic sentence.

> 아래 예는 "my family"라는 topic을 어떻게 narrowing하는지 보여줍니다.

Here is another example:

Suppose that your teacher asks you to write a paragraph describing one of the members of your family. Your task is to pick someone who you know well, and who you would like to write about. You should choose someone who is particularly interesting so that your reader will enjoy reading about that person too.

How do you know who to choose? Here are a couple of ideas that might help you!

1. Ask yourself who is going to be your **audience** for this paragraph. That is, who is going to be reading your paragraph?

    If your teacher is going to read the paragraph, then perhaps you might write about one of your parents and their special relationship with you.

    However, if your best friend is reading the paragraph, then maybe he or she would prefer to read about the antics(별난행동) of your little brother.

    In other words, choose the subject that your audience might like to hear about.

2. Decide what your **purpose** is in writing the paragraph. If you want to inform your reader, then writing about something more serious would likely be appropriate. However, if your purpose is to entertain your reader, then you might want to write something with some humor in it!

If you have been asked to write about a member of your family, you might ask yourself things like:

What person in my family do I admire the most?
Is there one person that I would enjoy writing about?
Who is the funniest person in the family?
Who is the most talented person in the family?
Who is the most unusual person in the family?

When you have decided on the person you want to write about, you have begun to narrow the topic. But you still need to do a bit more! Suppose you have decided to write about your brother. That is still a pretty big topic. You could probably write a book about him. So you need to narrow the topic even further.

To do this, you need to ask yourself why you want to write about him.

    a. What is special about my brother?
    b. What is there about my brother that might be of interest to the reader?

You might answer 'a' by saying that he is 'annoying'. And you might answer 'b' by saying that 'his behavior is rude'.

So you have now narrowed the topic even further. You are going to write about your brother, but you are going to focus on the fact that his behavior is annoying.

2. Topic and Controlling Idea

> 이 장에서는 "Narrowing the Topic"을 한 후 Topic Sentence를 만드는 과정을 공부합니다. Topic sentence는 "Topic"과 "Controlling Idea"로 구성됩니다. Topic은 글의 대상을 나타내며, Controlling Idea는 topic에 대해 글 쓰는 사람의 입장, 태도, 관점 등을 나타냅니다.

You are now ready to write your topic sentence. Writing the topic sentence forces you to take a stand and make a solid statement about your topic.

The simplest topic sentence that you could make about your brother might be:
    My Brother is annoying.

But that statement is still very general. There are probably a number of reasons why your brother is annoying, and there may not be enough room in a paragraph to discuss them all. You need to focus on one aspect of his annoying nature.

For example:
My Brother's rude behavior is annoying.

In this statement, you have identified a reason for your brother being annoying, and thus you have given your paragraph a better focus.

It is extremely important to write a good topic sentence because the topic sentence controls the direction of the paragraph.

There are really **two parts** to a strong topic sentence.

1) a statement of the topic
2) a statement of the writer's attitude toward the topic. This is called the controlling idea.

Look at this example:
My Brother's rude behavior is annoying.

In this topic sentence, **the topic** is *"My brother's rude behavior"*.
The writer's attitude toward the topic is that the behavior is *"annoying"* (the **controlling idea**).

The reader knows what the paragraph is going to be about, and he also knows how the writer feels about it.

> 아래의 예와 같이 하나의 topic에는 여러 개의 다른 controlling idea가 있습니다. Topic sentence에서 controlling idea는 paragraph가 어떤 내용으로 전개될지를 보여줍니다.

Look at the following topic and the four possible topic sentences.

Topic: University education
Possible Topic Sentences:
  a. A university education is necessary for success in today's society.
  b. A university education is highly overrated.
  c. University education demands strong study skills.
  d. University education is too expensive.

Although the topic is the same, each of these topic sentences will direct the paragraph in a very different direction.

In topic sentence (a), the topic is 'university education' and the controlling idea is that it is 'necessary for success in today's society".

> The controlling idea in (b): highly overrated
> The controlling idea in (c): demands strong study skills
> The controlling idea in (d): too expensive

You can see now how the topic may be the same, but the controlling idea will direct the focus of your paragraph. The controlling idea will let your reader know what the paragraph will be about.

Summary:

1) It is important to remember that your **topic** and your **topic sentence** are two different things.
2) The topic sentence must contain two things: the **topic** and the **controlling** idea; that is, your attitude/opinion toward the topic.
3) The **topic sentence** must be a complete sentence with a subject and a verb and it must express a complete thought.
4) Do not write "This paragraph is about…" or "I am going to write about…"

 Exercise 1

For each of the following topic sentences:
   a. Identify the topic.
   b. Identify the controlling idea.

1) My best friend is the funniest person I know.

   Topic:

   Controlling Idea:

2) I love to go skating in the winter.

   Topic:

   Controlling Idea:

3) Music makes my life enjoyable.

    Topic:

    Controlling Idea:

4) Working with animals is a rewarding experience.

    Topic:

    Controlling Idea:

5) The movie, "Mission Impossible" has outstanding special effects.

    Topic:

    Controlling Idea:

Exercise 2

For each of the following topics:
- a. Narrow the topic
- b. Choose a controlling idea
- c. Write the topic sentence

Example:
Topic: Popular Music
Narrowed Topic: Country Music
Controlling Idea: I like it a lot.
Topic Sentence: Country is my favorite type of music.

1. Topic: A person you admire

    Narrowed Topic:

    Controlling Idea:

    Topic Sentence:

2. Topic: A good memory

   Narrowed Topic:

   Controlling Idea:

   Topic Sentence:

3. Topic: Winter Sports

   Narrowed Topic:

   Controlling Idea:

   Topic Sentence:

4. Topic: Courage

   Narrowed Topic:

   Controlling Idea:

   Topic Sentence:

5. Topic: Cowardice

   Narrowed Topic:

   Controlling Idea:

   Topic Sentence:

✏️ Writing Exercise

> 이번 lesson에서 배운 것을 사용하여 아래 topic으로 3개의 paragraph writing을 합니다. 다음 장에 있는 Paragraph Planning Sheet를 작성한 후 writing을 하세요.

In this lesson, you have learned how to take a topic and narrow it, add a controlling idea and write the topic sentence. So, for the writing assignments in this lesson, you will be given the topics only. You will need to do the other steps. The attached planning sheets will help you organize your work.

Complete the planning sheets in the next pages, and then write three paragraphs. Each paragraph must be 125-150 words in length.

Here are the topics to choose from:

1) Computer games
2) Goals in life
3) Movies
4) A person you would like to meet.
5) My best friend
6) What I do to relax.
7) The best (worst) day of my life.

Paragraph Planning Sheet

Topic:

Narrowed Topic:

Controlling Idea:

Topic Sentence:

Ideas to support the topic sentence:

1.

2.

3.

Concluding Idea

Paragraph Planning Sheet

Topic:

Narrowed Topic:

Controlling Idea:

Topic Sentence:

Ideas to support the topic sentence:

1.

2.

3.

Concluding Idea

Paragraph Planning Sheet

Topic:

Narrowed Topic:

Controlling Idea:

Topic Sentence:

Ideas to support the topic sentence:

1.

2.

3.

Concluding Idea

Lesson 3 : Body of a Paragraph

> Body 부분은 topic sentence를 뒷받침하는 세부사항들을 포함합니다. 이번 lesson에서는 idea를 만들고, 취사선택, 그리고 배열(creating, selecting, dropping and arranging ideas)하는 방법을 공부합니다.

1. Creating Ideas

> Topic sentence가 정해진 후 다음 단계는 topic sentence를 뒷받침할 idea들을 만들어내는 것입니다. 이 idea들이 paragraph의 body 부분이 될 것입니다. Paragraph Planning 기법에 대해서는 Lesson 5에서 다시 자세히 다룰 것입니다.

Once you have decided on the topic sentence for your paragraph, you must create some ideas to support it.

1-1. Brainstorming

One good way to develop ideas is to **brainstorm**. This means that you will write all your ideas down on a piece of paper or on the computer. You will write down anything that you can think of that relates to your topic sentence.

Write down:

1) **examples** to prove your topic sentence
2) **facts** to support your topic sentence
3) **anecdotes**(일화), or small **stories** that prove your topic sentence
4) **details** to support the topic sentence

Many students try to skip this step, but in fact, it is one of the most important steps you can take to develop a strong paragraph. So, take the time to do this well. When your list is complete, then you can choose from your ideas to write your paragraph.

1–2. Questioning

One other method of creating ideas for the body of your paragraph is to ask yourself questions about the topic.

Try asking some of the following questions:

- *Why is this topic interesting?*
- *What can I teach my reader about this topic?*
- *How do I feel about this topic?*
- *What issues are there around this topic?*
- *Why would this be a good topic to write about?*

 ## Exercise 1

For each of the following topic sentences, create at least **four ideas** that could be used to support the topic sentence. Be sure to choose the best possible ideas.

1) Topic Sentence: Long life is not always a blessing.

    a.

    b.

    c.

    d.

2) Topic Sentence: Teens should not be given credit cards.

    a.

    b.

    c.

    d.

3) Topic Sentence: Most television shows are not worth watching.

   a.

   b.

   c.

   d.

2. Selecting/ Dropping/ Arranging Ideas

> Brainstorming을 통해 만들어진 Idea를 취사선택, 그리고 배열하는 방법을 공부합니다.

After you have brainstormed your ideas, you need to choose the ones that you want to select for your paragraph. You will want to choose the ideas that are the strongest, and that relate best to the topic sentence you have written. You should keep the facts, examples, and details that provide specific information about the topic sentence. You should get rid of any ideas that do not add anything new to the paragraph, or that just repeat the idea in the topic sentence.

If you are not sure which ideas to keep and which to drop, then underline the key words in the topic sentence to help you focus on the real point of your paragraph. Then, make sure that all the ideas you have chosen relate specifically to the point you are trying to make.

Now we are going to show you how to organize your ideas and how to arrange them effectively in your paragraph.

> 아래의 예는 Lesson 1에 나오는 "Winter" 제목의 paragraph에 대해 planning 과정에서 어떻게 brainstorming idea들을 취사선택하고 또 배열하는지를 보여줍니다.

Here is the brainstorming for the paragraph about *Winter* that you read in Lesson 1.

1) favorite time of the year because it snows
2) I like skating on the pond next door
3) driving is a little dangerous
4) dangers of avalanches (눈사태)

5) excitement
6) snowboarding
7) snow machines
8) mountain snow trails
9) some people play hockey
10) love the sound of the wind and the snow
11) hate to see winter end
12) bundled up in a lot of clothing
13) love to ski
14) feel like I have new energy

Step 1: Dropping Ideas

> 첫번째 단계는 brainstorming idea들 중에서 주제와 상관이 없는 idea를 삭제합니다. Paragraph의 주제는 "I like winter"이므로 winter에 대해 부정적인 idea들을 삭제합니다.

When the writer looked at his list, he saw that most of his ideas talked about things that he liked to do in the winter. So, he decided to get rid of some of the more negative aspects of winter.

Here is the list of items that the writer decided to delete from his points:

3) driving is a little dangerous
4) dangers of avalanches
12) bundled up in a lot of clothing

Step 2: Grouping Ideas

> 다음 단계는 서로 공통점이 있는 idea들을 grouping합니다.

The next step was to **combine** some of his ideas into groups that related to each other. The ideas in each group must have something in common; that is, they must be related in some specific way.

Here are the groups he decided on.

Group 1: This group describes the ice sports
2) I like skating on the pond next door
9) some people play hockey

Group 2: This group describes how he feels
   5) excitement
   14) feel like I have new energy

Group 3: This group describes snow sports
   6) snowboarding
   10) love the sound of the wind and snow
   13) love to ski

Group 4: This group describes the motorized snow sport
   7) snow machines
   8) mountain snow trails

Group 5
   1) favorite time of year
   11) hate to see winter end

When the writer looked at Group 5, he realized that he was expressing his feelings about winter in a very general way. He decided that the 'favorite time of year' was an excellent way to begin and that 'hate to see winter end' would be a good way to conclude his paragraph.

Step 3: Organizing Ideas

> 마지막 단계는 각 idea group들을 paragraph 내에서 어떻게 배열할 것인지를 결정합니다. Idea를 배열하는 구체적인 방법은 Lesson 4 에서 자세히 다루도록 하겠습니다.

Now he needed to decide how to organize his paragraph. What idea should come first?

He looked at the groups again and decided that Group 2 would be an excellent way to support the feelings he stated in the topic sentence.

Since Groups 3 and 4 both talked about snow sports, he decided not to put them together in the paragraph. Instead, he would put Group 1 in between so that the organization would look like this:

Topic Sentence:	*Winter is my favorite time of year.*
Support for topic sentence:	*Group 2*
First Point:	*Group 3 (Snow Sports)*

Second Point: *Group 1 (Ice Sports)*
Third Point: *Group 4 (Motorized Snow Sports)*
Final (Concluding Sentence): *I am always sad to see the end of winter.*

Here is the paragraph that he wrote:

> Winter is my favorite time of year. When the snow begins to fall, I feel a new energy and excitement. Soon I will be able to ski and snowboard on the mountains. There is nothing more beautiful than a day on the slopes with the wind in my face and the sound of the snow beneath my boards. When I am not skiing, I am skating on the pond on my neighbor's farm. There is always a group of enthusiastic hockey players ready for a game. One of the best times of the winter is when we go for a weekend trip on our snow machines. We follow the ready made paths up into the mountains, and there, when the snow is good, we blaze new trails through the forests and valleys. I am always sad to see the end of winter!

3. Paragraph Unity

> Unity는 writing에서 각 idea들 간의 일관성을 의미합니다. 즉 paragraph의 모든 문장들은 topic sentence에 대한 것이어야 합니다. 흔히 쉬운 사항으로 생각하여 간과하는 경우가 많은데 실제로 고급 수준 학생들의 essay에서도 topic에서 벗어난 (off topic), 즉 unified가 되지 않은 경우가 흔히 지적됩니다.

The word "unity" means "togetherness". When we apply the word to writing, it describes a piece of writing that is "on topic". A unified piece does not stray from its topic. The details in each paragraph individually related to the topic sentence, and all the paragraphs in an essay relate to the thesis. In simple terms, **each sentence must, in some way, clearly relate back to the topic being discussed in the essay.**

Examples of a paragraph which are NOT unified:

1) Topic sentence: *Driving in the country is a very pleasant experience.*

> Driving in the country is a very pleasant experience. On a sunny day, there is nothing nicer than opening the car windows and breathing in the fresh country air. The natural smells of the countryside invigorate the body and the mind. I like the

smell of my flower garden too. As well, a drive in the country is educational. One can see birds and animals that are not found in the city. Learning their names adds to one's knowledge of nature. Blue jays are my favorite birds. They are big birds with very strange cries. They sound a bit like crows. Finally driving in the country relieves stress. There is no traffic and the pace of life is slower. A country drive is a great way to relax.

In the paragraph above, there are four underlined sentences which do not support the topic sentence (not unified).

2) Topic sentence: *Young people today are finding that making a living is a difficult task.*

　　　Young people today are finding that making a living is a difficult task. A young person without a Grade-12 education is forced to accept minimum-wage jobs which demand a great deal of effort, but pay little in return. Not everyone can get a Grade-12 education because the work is hard in the upper grades. As well, young people cannot find full-time jobs, and part-time work pays very little. Employers do not want to pay the benefits required for full-time employees, and therefore they tend to hire several people to work part-time with minimal numbers of hours and thus, small paychecks. That is really not fair to young people. Finally, young people tend to be hired only for seasonal work - summer holidays and Christmas - and even at these times, they find that hourly wages are very low. The jobs end with the season, and again these young people are without work. The government must step in and stop this.

There are three underlined sentences in the above paragraph which do not support the topic sentence (not unified).

 ## Exercise 2

Sometimes ideas may seem to support a topic, but they really don't. In each of the following, you will find ideas that look right, but are not appropriate in the context.

For each of the following, carefully read the topic sentence, then choose the <u>three</u> ideas which best support it.

1) <u>Topic Sentence:</u> Diet foods are often unpleasant to eat.
　　　1. Rice crackers are dry and tasteless.
　　　2. You don't feel full on diet foods.

3. Diet soft drinks have an unnatural sickly sweetness.
4. Diet foods are low in calories.
5. Diet ice cream tastes thin and insipid.
6. Eating too much diet food is often harmful to your health.
7. Aspartame is a dangerous sugar substitute.

2) <u>Topic Sentence:</u> Driving while intoxicated could change your life.

1. You could have an accident and be permanently disabled.
2. Drunks often fall asleep while driving.
3. You might end up in jail with a criminal record.
4. You might end up with life-long guilt if you hurt someone in an accident.
5. Alcohol gives people bad judgement.
6. Drunks often end up slurring their words.
7. Drunks spend a lot of money on alcohol.

Exercise 3

For each of the following paragraphs, underline sentences that should be omitted to keep the paragraph unified.

1) The worst part of living in a city is the noise. Every day there is traffic, and the roar of cars and trucks with their loud mufflers, screeching brakes and blowing horns is deafening. Truck horns are the worst. Their air-powered honks could wake the dead! Some trucks have two kinds of horns. Another kind of noise that is heard in the city is the sound of emergency vehicles. Sirens for police, ambulances, and fire trucks blare through the air both night and day. Their piercing sounds are hard on the ears and the nerves. The police sirens have changed in the last few years. Finally, there is the noise of the crowds. In malls, on the streets, in restaurants, bars, and sports stadiums, there is always the sound of people talking, laughing, shouting and screaming. And most cities have lots of malls for people to visit.

2) The "Harry Potter" books by J.K. Rowling are excellent reading for children. First of all, they have creative and fascinating plots. The stories all involve magic, which is always exciting for children. There are spells, monsters, magical animals and wizardry, all ingredients for good reading. Many children would like to be able to do magic. As

well, the books have main characters who are in the same age group as the readers. Children can relate to the characters and so the books are more understandable and realistic for young readers. But kids should not think that Harry Potter is real. Lastly, the books have a good level of vocabulary which is both challenging and accessible to a number of different age groups. The language level in the novels is educational rather than condescending. Thus, a child's language level can improve by reading the books. Sometimes a child will need to ask a parent for the meaning of a word in the novel.

3) One strong argument in favor of having uniforms in schools is that they reduce superficial competition between students. Hair styles and jewelry might become focal points for competitiveness among girls, but schools can impose rules to restrict hair fashion and accessories. By implementing uniforms, schools encourage their students to focus on healthy and meaningful competition, whether academic or athletic or both. Opponents may object that uniforms stifle the creativity students express through their clothing choices. However, this argument defines creative expression too narrowly and shallowly. It is important to encourage creativity. In fact, by directing students away from fashion, school uniforms prompt them to consider other means of expressing their individuality, such as visual arts, dance, music, theatre, culinary creations, or any one of a multitude of other activities. Uniforms promote healthy competitive student interactions while encouraging young people to engage in more intelligent and significant creative self-expression.

✏️ Writing Exercise

> 이번 lesson의 writing exercise는 지금까지와는 다른 방법으로 합니다. 하나의 topic에서 3개의 topic sentence들을 선정하여 3개의 paragraph를 작성합니다. 또한 첨부된 paragraph planning sheet를 이용하여 이번 lesson에서 배운 creating, selecting, dropping, grouping 그리고 arranging ideas를 직접 순서대로 해보도록 합니다.

In this lesson, you will be writing **three paragraphs** as you have done in previous lessons, but you are going to do something a little different this time.

You are going to write **three paragraphs** on the **same** topic. That means that you will have to develop **three different topic sentences for the topic**. Since the paragraphs are all separate, they do not have to have any relationship to each other. Each paragraph must be 125-150 words in length.

1) Write **five** topic sentences for the following topic.

   Topic: *Friends*
   Possible topic sentences:

   1.

   2.

   3.

   4.

   5.

2) Choose **three** topic sentences that you believe will make the best paragraphs. Then follow the following stages using the Paragraph Planning Sheets.

   a. List all the ideas you have about the topic sentence.
   b. Delete any points that do not apply to the topic sentence.
   c. Put your related points into groups.
   d. Organize the groups into the order in which you will discuss them in the paragraph.

Paragraph Planning Sheet

1) Topic Sentence:

2) List of Ideas
    a.
    b.
    c.
    d.
    e.
    f.
    g.
    h.
    i.
    j.
    k.
    l.

3) Deleted Ideas

4) Groups of Ideas

    Group 1
    Group 2
    Group 3
    Group 4

5) List the order that you would use for the groups in the paragraph:

Paragraph Planning Sheet

1) Topic Sentence:

2) List of Ideas
   a.
   b.
   c.
   d.
   e.
   f.
   g.
   h.
   i.
   j.
   k.
   l.

3) Deleted Ideas

4) Groups of Ideas

   Group 1
   Group 2
   Group 3
   Group 4

5) List the order that you would use for the groups in the paragraph:

Paragraph Planning Sheet

1) Topic Sentence:

2) List of Ideas
   a.
   b.
   c.
   d.
   e.
   f.
   g.
   h.
   i.
   j.
   k.
   l.

3) Deleted Ideas

4) Groups of Ideas

   Group 1
   Group 2
   Group 3
   Group 4

5) List the order that you would use for the groups in the paragraph:

Lesson 4 : Organizing a Paragraph

> 이번 Lesson에서는 paragraph에서 idea들을 배열하는 방법에 대해 공부합니다. Idea를 배열하는 방식에는 흔히 다음의 3가지가 있습니다. Paragraph의 내용에 따라 적절한 방법을 적용하세요.
> – Time Order (시간/연대순)
> – Emphatic Order (중요도순)
> – Space Order (공간/위치순)

When we talk about effective writing, we often think first about elements like word choice, grammar and mechanics, and content or evidence. But a really important part of effective writing is clear, logical organization.

When things are laid out in some sort of order, we can work with them more easily. If we can impose some kind of order on information, the information is easier to talk about, easier to understand, and easier to remember. If you choose a clear, recognizable pattern (for a single paragraph, and also for a whole essay), you find it easier to select details and choose transitions, and you also help your reader discover relationships that connect things, that make things seem more coherent.

There are three common methods of organizing the ideas in an essay or a paragraph, **"Time Order"**, **"Emphatic Order (Order of Importance)"** and **"Space Order"**.

These are not the only organizational methods, of course, but they are useful ones with which to begin.

1. Time Order

> Time order는 시간순 (또는 역순)으로 idea들을 배열하는 방법입니다. First, then, next 등의 time signal을 사용합니다.

There are many times that details can be arranged in your writing according to the sequence in which they occur. You can arrange ideas from past to present, or present to past depending on your purpose in the essay or paragraph. Most stories, histories, and instructions follow the logical order of time.

Words and phrases such as **"first, next, then, to begin with, finally"** are the signals which indicate these time sequences.

> **Example:**
> *Thesis: To be a successful cook, you need to be well-prepared before you begin.*
> 1. ***To begin with***, *be sure your utensils are clean and ready.*
> 2. ***Next***, *get all your ingredients measured.*
> 3. ***Finally***, *make sure that you have read and understand each step of the recipe.*

You can also use these sorts of words and phrases within paragraphs to improve the flow of your ideas. Showing the chronological connections between the events or actions you are describing helps your readers to envision them and follow your train of thought.

Time Order Transitions:

then	next	later	meanwhile	when
now	soon	since	in the meantime	shortly
immediately	today	before	afterward	finally
lastly	last of all	the final		

Exercise 1

Here is one supporting paragraph from an essay. Look for the **"time signals"**.

> Next, get your utensils ready. If you are baking a cake, you will require items for mixing the batter. Most likely you will use an electric mixer, but you will also need a spoon, a spatula, and a mixing bowl. Then you should organize your baking ingredients. You will need flour, eggs, salt, baking powder, and milk or water as the recipe requires. After you have utensils and ingredients, you will need to organize your baking tins. You will need two tins for a layer cake, a large tin for a slab cake, or a tube tin for an angel food cake. Finally, be sure that you have turned the oven on to warm it up to the correct temperature to cook your perfect cake.

List the **time signals** used in the previous paragraph:

_____, _____, _____, _____

 Exercise 2

Arrange each set of sentences into a logical time order. Number the sentences in the correct time order in which they would appear in a paragraph. Look at 'time' words to give you clues as to the order

1) _____ First, go to a quiet spot in your home or library.
   _____ Next, be sure that you will not be interrupted.
   _____ Finally, sit on a straight backed chair and begin.
   _____ Then, remove all extraneous material from your study area.
   _____ Experts tell us that there are several correct steps to effective studying.

2) _____ In 1944, Jane was born in Quebec, Canada
   _____ Before her first birthday, her parents knew that she was special because she could already read many words.
   _____ Her last novel was published in 1974 when she was thirty years old.
   _____ In her long career, Jane Bond published 41 novels, over half of which have become classics.
   _____ Her first book came in 1954 when she was only 10, and she became an overnight success and an instant celebrity.
   _____ Despite her efforts to write, Jane has not been able to complete one novel since 1974.

3) Thesis: Going to the movies is not a pleasant experience.

   _____ When I go to the movies, I am frustrated when I have to stand in line for tickets.
   _____ Upon leaving the theatre, I can never find my car in the parking lot.
   _____ During the movie, I am annoyed by people who make comments about the action on the screen.
   _____ Once I reach the theatre, I have trouble finding a place to park.

4) Thesis: Applying for my first job was a stressful experience.

   _____ I couldn't find the building where I was to have the interview.
   _____ The dress that I had planned to wear to the interview was dirty.
   _____ When I left, I forgot to leave my resume with the interviewers.
   _____ The interviewers asked several questions that took me by surprise.

2. Emphatic Order (Order of Importance)

> Emphatic order는 중요도 순으로 idea들을 배열하는 방법입니다. 3개의 배열 방법이 있습니다.

Order of importance is one of the most frequently-employed organizing principles used in paragraphs and essays.

This type of writing organization can be used in three ways;

1) From the **least** important to the **most**
2) From the **most** important to the **least**
3) **Second most** important at the beginning, the **lease** in the middle and the **most** important at the end

1) Least Important First

This type of organization takes the reader from the least important idea to the most important idea. The ideas build in importance, holding the reader's attention. The best is saved for the last. By saving the most important idea to the last, you work your paragraph to a climax.

2) Most Important First

In this type of organization, the most important idea is stated first and the least important idea is stated last. This method is used most often in newspaper articles. This way if the reader does not finish the article he/she will still know the most important details. This method grabs the reader's attention in the beginning, but it does not work very well in holding the reader's attention clear to the end.

3) Second most important - the least - the most

Readers usually give most attention to what comes at the beginning and the end, and least attention to what is in the middle. In this pattern, then, you decide what is the second most important and put it at the beginning; next you choose what is the most important and put it at the end; the less important items are then arranged in the middle. In this way, your essay gets a strong start and an even stronger finish.

Emphatic Order Transitions:

furthermore	in addition	second	another	in the second place
likewise	also	additionally	moreover	above all
most important	most of all			

Exercise 3

Read the following paragraph:

Honesty is one of the greatest virtues in society. First of all, being honest is good for the soul. Honest people do not carry guilt because they have not kept secrets from anyone and therefore from themselves. More importantly, honesty keeps the lines of communication open. Being able to tell the truth prevents people from building up secrets which create barriers in relationships. But most importantly, honesty allows people to deal with themselves and others on a clear footing, without pretense. In every situation in life - family, marriage, and business partnerships - being honest means that the relationship can thrive. No one will 'second guess' the motives of others since the truth is already known. Honesty is definitely an important quality in any society.

1) Write down the topic sentence of this paragraph.

2) What is the most important idea in the paragraph?

3) What words does the writer use to introduce the most important idea in the paragraph?

4) What is the second most important idea in the paragraph?

5) What words does the writer use to introduce the second most important idea in the paragraph?

6) What is the least important idea in the paragraph?

 Exercise 4

Read the following paragraph:

When the tsunami of December 2004 hit the coast of Indonesia, the results were horrific. Over 300,000 lives were lost in the destruction, leaving children without parents and parents without their children. The loss of life was equivalent to the population of a good sized North American city. As well, the inhabitants lost their homes which were swept away into the sea. Furniture and personal belongings were gone with the huge wave which crashed onto the beach. Another result of the tsunami was economic. Until Indonesian resorts can rebuild, the country will be without its many tourists. Instead it is filled with aid workers and those who simply want to see the devastated countryside. The tsunami brought death and destruction to this tiny tropical paradise.

1) What is the topic sentence of the paragraph?

2) What is the most important idea in the paragraph?

3) At what point in the paragraph is the most important idea stated?

4) What is the least important idea in the paragraph?

5) At what point in the paragraph is the least important idea stated?

3. Space Order

> Space order는 무비 카메라가 움직이듯 대상의 상하, 좌우, 또는 전후로 움직이면서 묘사하는 방법입니다. 이 방법은 어떤 대상을 묘사하는 Essay에 적합한 방법입니다.

When you write descriptions, the most logical order to use is space order. This order arranges ideas as if you were looking through the eye of a movie camera. When you describe, you can move from bottom to top, left to right, front to back, back to front and so on. Generally paragraphs that are written to persuade or argue do not make great use of space order. However, it is the best order to use when describing someone or something.

In this order, you will use words that direct the reader to the various locations in the scene. Words and phrases such as **to the left**, **to the right**, **above**, **below**, **around**, **across**, **inside** are used in the space order.

Look at the following paragraph which uses space order.

> When I look out the window of my living room, I see the most amazing scene. In the foreground is my garden, alive with the colors of spring. Pathways wind around the flower beds and disappear into groves of pine trees that cluster on both sides of the garden. One path winds down the hill below the garden. It disappears over the small hill that dips down toward the lake. The lake is blue and shimmers in the morning light. Across the lake I can see the mountains rising out of the blue. To the left is a small ranch and to the right, a road is visible, snaking up the mountainside toward the summit which is still capped in snow. My eyes return to my garden again and I smile in the knowledge that I am part of this beautiful landscape.

 **Writing Exercise**

You will write **three** paragraphs of 125-150 words each. Use the attached Paragraph Planning Sheets to help you organize your ideas.

Writing 1
Write a paragraph on one of the following topics using **time order**.

    Topics: The first hour of your average day
                    The most unforgettable event in your life

Writing 2
Write a paragraph on one of the following topics using **space order**.

    Topics: Your house
                    Your classroom

Writing 3
Write a paragraph on one of the following topics using the **emphatic order**, but you decide whether you will arrange the ideas "from most important to least important", "least important to most important" or "second most important at the beginning, the lease in the middle and the most important at the end".

    Topics: The day that everything went wrong.
                    The strangest looking person that I ever saw

Paragraph Planning Sheet

Topic:

Narrowed Topic:

Controlling Idea:

Topic Sentence:

Order of Ideas:

Ideas to support the topic sentence:

1.

2.

3.

Concluding Idea

Paragraph Planning Sheet

Topic:

Narrowed Topic:

Controlling Idea:

Topic Sentence:

Order of Ideas:

Ideas to support the topic sentence:

1.

2.

3.

Concluding Idea

Paragraph Planning Sheet

Topic:

Narrowed Topic:

Controlling Idea:

Topic Sentence:

Order of Ideas:

Ideas to support the topic sentence:

1.

2.

3.

Concluding Idea

Lesson 5 : Paragraph Planning

> 글을 쓰기 전에 idea들을 만들어내는 planning 과정은 흔히 간과되고 있습니다. 많은 학생들이 planning에 충분한 시간을 할애하지 않고, 바로 writing을 시작하는 것이 시간을 절약하는 것이라 생각합니다. 그러나 실은 그 반대입니다. Writing plan은 글쓰는 전체 시간을 오히려 단축시켜주며 글의 완성도를 높여줍니다.
>
> Paragraph planning에는 여러 방법이 있습니다. 이번 lesson에서는 Linear Diagramming과 Continuous Timed Writing의 예를 공부합니다.

Sometimes it is hard to think of good ideas to write about. There are many ways to discover these ideas. In this lesson, we will show you two brainstorming techniques called **Linear Diagramming and Continuous Timed Writing**.

The paragraph planning allows you a chance to organize your ideas before you write. If you know exactly what you want to write about before you begin, you will find that it is easier to complete the writings. You will not waste time thinking about things as you write, or changing things around. If you complete your planning carefully, making as many changes as you want before you begin to write, you will find that your work proceeds much more smoothly.

1. Linear Diagramming

> Linear Diagram으로 paragraph planning하는 과정을 공부합니다. 이 방법은 topic에 대해 3개의 main idea를 만들고 각 main idea마다 다시 3개의 supporting detail을 만드는 전통적인 planning 방법입니다.

Here is an example of a **Linear Diagram**.

Let's say that your topic is *"The most important things a parent can teach a child."* Put that topic on the line in the first column.

Then, look at the diagram. There are **three lines in the second column**. On these lines, you are going to put the lessons that you want to talk about. So, let's fill in those lines now. Be sure to think about these ideas very carefully since you will write your paragraph using these ideas.

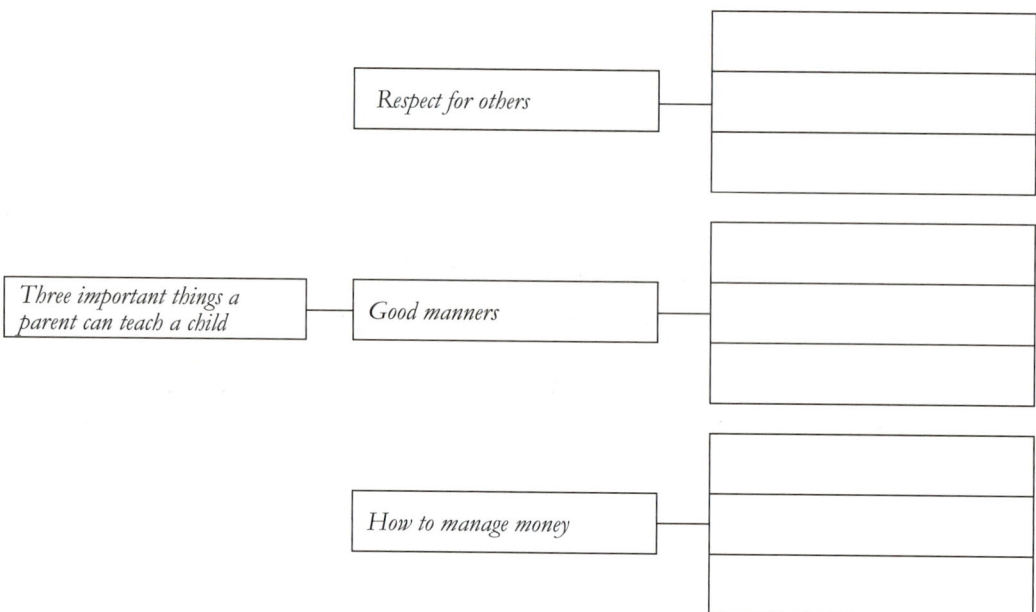

Now you have three ideas to write about. But if you were going to write a paragraph about these ideas, you would need to add more details to make your paragraph interesting, and to persuade your reader that your opinion is a good one. So, let's use the final column to write down some details about each of the ideas that you have listed. You will have **three details** for each idea that you have listed.

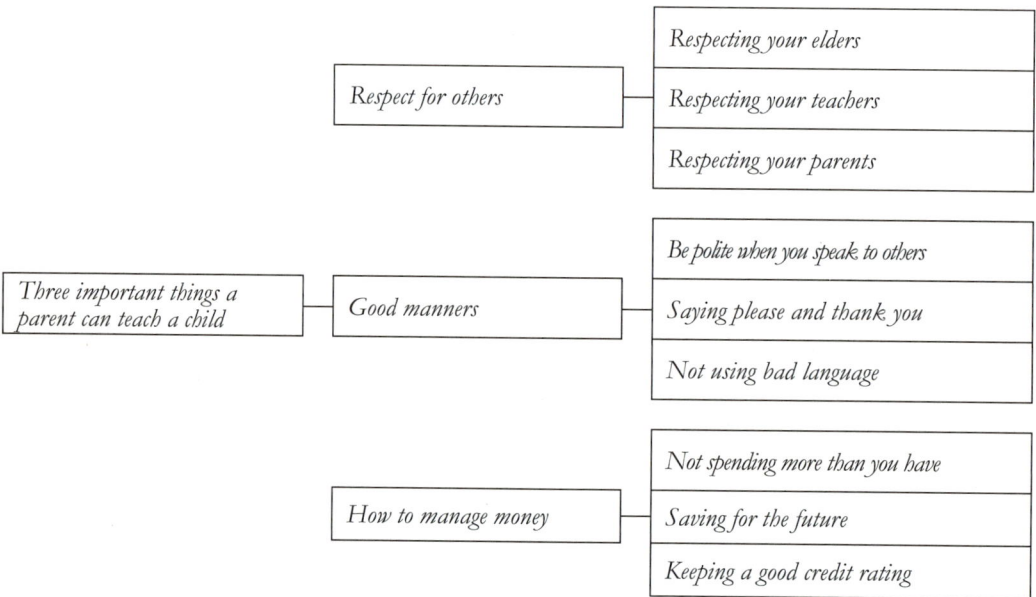

Now you have completed the entire Linear Diagram and you have lots of things to write about! Let's take those ideas and the details, and write a paragraph using all of them.

Here is a possible paragraph. We have shown you the ideas from the linear diagram in **bold letters**.

*Parents teach their children many things, but there are three things that I believe are **the most important lessons** that parents need to teach their children. First of all, they must teach them to **respect others**. The children need to learn to have respect for people who are older than they are. They must also learn to respect their teachers at school as well as their parents at home. Secondly, a good parent **teaches** a child to have **good manners**. Children must learn to be **polite** when they speak to others. They must learn to say **'please'** when they want something and **'thank you'** when they receive it. Parents must also insist that children **never use bad language** when they speak. Thirdly, a parent must teach a child to **manage money** well. One of the most important things a child needs to learn is **not to spend more money** than they have. They must also learn to **save for the future** and to maintain a **good credit rating**. These are three of the most important things a parent can teach a child.*

Let's do another example of a linear diagram.

Imagine this time that the topic is *"The places I would like to visit in the world"*. We'll begin again by putting the title in the first column. Then, let's add our choices. I know three places that I would like to go, so let's put those in the second column.

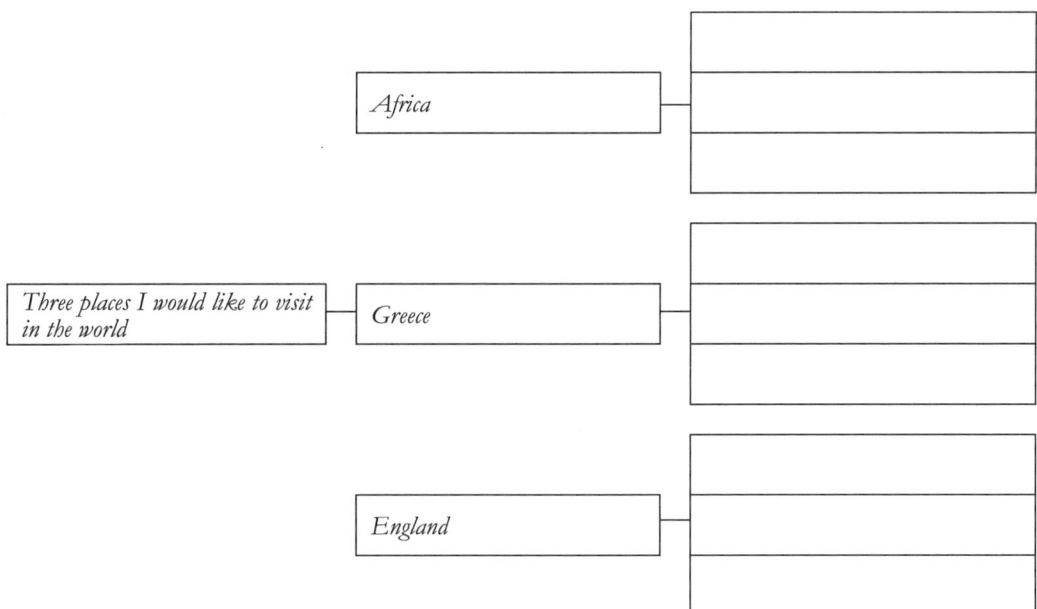

Lesson 5: Paragraph Planning **65**

Now I have to add some details. I ask myself why I want to visit those places, and those are the **details** that I will add. So, let's fill in the third column.

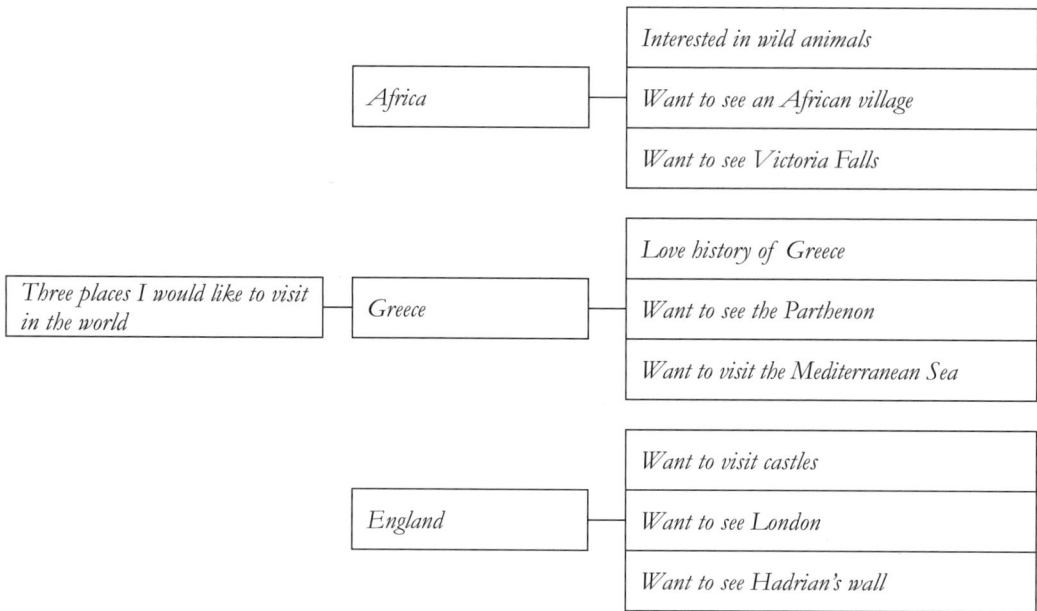

We have all our ideas and our details, so now we are ready to write the paragraph. We will **bold** all the ideas from the Linear Diagram so that you can see how they have been included in the paragraph.

> I have been to a lot of interesting places, but there are still **three places I want to see**. First of all, I want to go to **Africa**. I would love to see **wild animals**, especially lions and elephants. As well, I want to visit a real **African village** and see how the people live. But most of all, I want to see the famous **Victoria Falls**, which is the largest waterfall in the world. Another place that I want to visit is **Greece**. I have always been fascinated with ancient **history of that area**, and I would like to see the places I have read about. The **Parthenon** is the building that I want to see the most, but I also want to spend some time relaxing by the **Mediterranean Sea**. Lastly, I would like to go to **England**. I have always enjoyed learning about the royal family, so I would like to see some **castles**. I'd also like to shop in **London** and make a trip to the countryside to visit **Hadrian's Wall**. I hope that I will have a chance to see all of these places in my lifetime.

 **Writing Exercise 1**

Now it is your turn to write!

Use the following **Linear Diagram** to find ideas for the following topic.

Topic: *There are three things that I want to do in my lifetime.*

Here is the Linear Diagram for you to complete. We have added the topic in the first column.

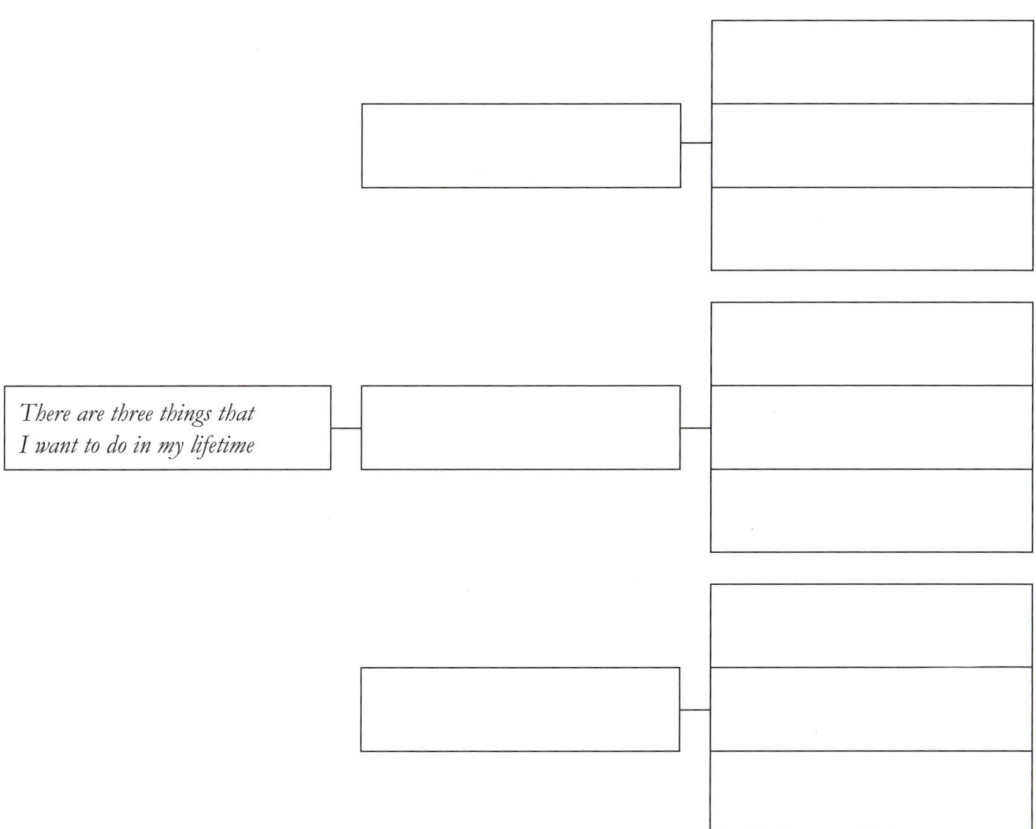

Now, use the information from your linear diagram to write the paragraph. Make sure that you include all the information and that your paragraph must be 125-150 words in length.

Write your paragraph.

2. Continuous Timed Writing

> Topic이 주어지고 writing을 시작하려 할 때 무엇을 쓸지 몰라 시작을 할 수 없는 경우가 있습니다. Continuous Timed Writing은 이런 경우에 도움을 주는 방법입니다. 이 방법으로 효과를 보는 학생이 많으니 꼭 한번 시도해보기 바랍니다. Continuous Timed Writing은 2단계로 이루어집니다.

In this lesson, we will show you a new way to brainstorm. This method of finding ideas is called **Continuous Timed Writing**.

Sometimes, when we sit down to write, it is hard to get started. We look at a blank page, or a blank computer screen, and it is difficult to put the first words down. Using the Continuous Timed Writing method may be the help you need to get started!

To use this method, you have to know your topic. If you don't have a topic, you will need to find one before this method will work for you. But once you have a topic, the process is very simple. At the end of the process, if you do it correctly, you will have a completed paragraph.

Stage 1

> 첫번째 단계입니다. 시간은 5분에서 15분 사이로 본인에게 적절한 시간을 정하세요. 영어로 쓰는 것이 원칙이나 단어가 생각나지 않을 경우 한글을 같이 써도 무방합니다.

1) Put the topic in the centre top of a piece of paper or a Word Processing document.
2) You will need a timer that you can set for 5 minutes.
3) When the timer is set, you will begin to write about your topic.
    a. You will not rush the writing.
    b. You will write everything that you can think about for your topic.
    c. Do not spend time correcting spelling or grammar. You will have a chance to correct these when you write the final copy of your work.
    d. The key to success is to write constantly without rushing and without stopping.

4) At the end of 5 minutes, you stop writing.

At this point, you have done **one-half of the process**. So, let's give you an example of the first five steps of Continuous Timed Writing.

Example:

Mary has been asked to write about her favorite time of year. She has chosen to write about 'Summer'

Mary is going to use the computer to brainstorm her topic using the Continuous Timed Writing technique. She opens a new Word Processing Document and puts her title at the top. Then, she sets her timer for five minutes and begins to write. Here is what she has written in five minutes:

Summer

I love summer the most. In the summer, I go swimming, camping and hiking. Our family goes on a camping trip and we spend a lot of time outside. Whenever I think of summer, I think of sunshine, water, and sports. Some of the sports I like are tennis, waterskiing, and baseball. I also like summer because there is no school. In summer we like to go on vacation to our cottage at the lake. We also go camping. There are a lot of wonderful things about summer. I don't like winter because it is too cold. I think spring is okay and so is fall, but I like the summer because it is warm. Summer is the best time of year because I am free to do the things that I enjoy in life.

In five minutes, she has written down a lot of her ideas about her topic. The ideas are not organized, and she needs to add some more details, but she has made a really good start on her writing. So, where does she go from here?

We said earlier that this writing was only one-half of the Continuous Timed Writing technique. Here are the rest of the steps.

Stage 2

> 두 번째 단계입니다. 첫 단계와 같이 시간은 5분에서 15분 사이로 본인에게 적절한 시간을 정하세요. 첫 번째 단계에서 한글로 쓴게 있으면 영어로 고칩니다. 두 번째 단계에서는 가능한 한 영어로 쓰도록 합니다. 두 번째 단계에서는, 첫 단계 writing에서 가장 흥미로운 문장을 topic sentence로 정하고 다시 writing을 합니다.

5) Now, read what you have written.
6) **Choose a sentence** that you think is the best. It may contain the best idea; it might be the most interesting; or it might be the most creative. Underline the sentence you chose.
7) Once you have decided on the sentence, write your sentence on the paper, or type it into the Word Processing document. This sentence will be the first sentence of your new writing.

8) Set your timer for another 5 minutes.
9) Using the sentence that you chose as your **topic sentence**, write constantly and without rushing for five more minutes. Be sure that all your ideas follow logically from the first sentence.
10) After you have completed the writing, check your work for spelling and grammar errors.

Here is Mary's first writing. She chose the last sentence of her writing and underlined it.

> *I love summer the most. In the summer, I go swimming, camping and hiking. Our family goes on a camping trip and we spend a lot of time outside. Whenever I think of summer, I think of sunshine, water, and sports. Some of the sports I like are tennis, waterskiing, and baseball. I also like summer because there is no school. In summer we like to go on vacation to our cottage at the lake. We also go camping. There are a lot of wonderful things about summer. I don't like winter because it is too cold. I think spring is okay and so is fall, but I like the summer because it is warm. <u>Summer is the best time of year because I am free to do the things that I enjoy in life.</u>*

Now, Mary is opening a new Word Processing document and she is typing the sentence she chose. *"Summer is the best time of year because I am free to do the things that I enjoy in life"*.

Mary sets her timer and begins to write. The following is what she wrote in the five minutes.

> ### *Summer*
> *Summer is the best time of year because I am free to do the things that I enjoy in life. In the summer, there is no school, so I can do a lot of things without worrying about doing homework. I love to go to our cottage at the lake. We can go waterskiing and swimming every day. Our family also likes to camp. We go to a special campground in the mountains where there are lots of hiking trails. When we aren't at the cottage or at the camp, we stay home and I play baseball and tennis. Summer is warm and it is my favorite time of year.*

This time, Mary's writing is much more organized. All the ideas relate to the first sentence that she chose from her original **Continuous Timed Writing**. Now, she has a really good paragraph about her topic, 'Summer' and it only took her ten minutes of writing and thinking!

✏️ Writing Exercise 2

Now, you are going to try out the process.

The topic that you are going to write about is *'An Ideal Friend'*.

1) Write the word *'An Ideal Friend'* in the centre top of a piece of paper or a new Word Processing document.
2) You will need a timer.
3) Here is a reminder of what you must do:
    a. You will not rush the writing.
    b. You will write everything that you can think about for your topic.
    c. Do not spend time correcting spelling or grammar. You will have a chance to correct these when you write the final copy of your work.
4) Stop writing when the 5-15 minutes is up.

Start your writing!

At this point, you have done **one-half of the process**. So, let's continue.

5) Now, read what you have written.
6) Choose a sentence that you think is the best. It may contain the best idea; it might be the most interesting; or it might be the most creative. Underline the sentence you chose.
7) Once you have decided on the sentence, write your sentence on the paper, or type it into the Word Processing document. This sentence will be the first sentence of your new writing.
8) Set your timer for another 5-15 minutes.
9) Using the sentence that you chose as your topic sentence, write constantly and without rushing for 5-15 minutes. Be sure that all your ideas follow logically from the first sentence.
10) After you have completed the writing, check your work for spelling and grammar errors.

Lesson 6 :
Editing and Revising

> Essay를 쓴 후에 검토하고 수정하는 작업은 중요합니다. 이번 lesson에서는 하나의 paragraph가 어떻게 editing되고 revising되는지 단계별로 공부합니다. Revising은 ARRRP라는 다섯 단계로 이루어집니다.
> - **A** : Adding Ideas
> - **R** : Removing Unnecessary Ideas
> - **R** : Rewording
> - **R** : Reordering
> - **P** : Proofreading

Often students believe that once they have written a paragraph, it is finished. However, one try is never enough! Great authors write and rewrite their work many times. It is not unusual for an author to rewrite a story fifteen or twenty times before he is satisfied with it! So, if it takes a great author several attempts, then it certainly will take students more than one try!

The first draft of a paragraph usually states the essential ideas that the writer wants to convey to the reader. But there are many things to consider.

- Is the paragraph organized as well as it can be?
- Are the details clear and concise but interesting?
- Has the writer used all the best words?
- Is there anything that needs to be added to make the ideas clearer?
- Are there any details that could be left out?
- Is there any repetition of ideas in the paragraph?
- Is the spelling correct?
- Are there any grammar errors?
- Are there any sentences that need to be rewritten for clarity?

These are questions that need to be asked before a final copy of a piece of writing is prepared.

The revision process can be identified by the following letters, **ARRRP**. Here is what that stands for:

A :   **Add**
R :   **Remove**

R :   Reword
R :   Reorder
P :   Proofread

1. Adding Ideas

> 아래 paragraph는 supporting detail이 충분하지 않습니다. 불충분한 supporting detail을 보완하기 위해 detail들이 add되는 과정을 보여줍니다.
> Paragraph에서 topic sentence를 뒷받침하는 idea의 개수와 각 idea를 설명하는 supporting detail의 개수는 해당 paragraph의 topic에 따라 결정됩니다. 그러나 일반적으로 topic sentence를 충분히 뒷받침하고 설명하려면 3개 이상의 idea와 각 idea에 대해 3개 이상의 supporting detail을 필요로 합니다.

Read the following paragraph carefully.

There is a great deal of talk today about Global Warming. Scientists are not in agreement about this phenomenon. Some feel that human beings are not responsible for the climate change that we have been experiencing over the past century, whereas other scientists claim that human beings are doing things that are definitely responsible for the warming trend. Politicians are also interested in Global Warming. But whatever scientists tell us we cannot ignore the fact that our climate is changing and we need to look at the reasons for this. In the past few years, there has been a growing awareness of the potential problems caused by Global Warming. Melting the icecaps too quickly can produce flooding, and in time could destroy our access to clean water. Sometimes people exaggerate the changes in the climate. One of the great problems of Global Warming involves food supply. Although growing seasons may be increased, there is a danger that the world could change the kinds of foods that we grow now. Global Warming is a concern and people must learn what they can do to stop it before it becomes a real problem.

Let's examine this paragraph. This paragraph would look like this if we put it into a Writing Plan:

<u>Writing Plan</u>

The topic: *Global Warming*
Topic sentence: *There is a great deal of talk today about Global Warming*

The three ideas:
> Idea #1: *Scientists are not in agreement*
> > – *Some scientists do not believe in Global Warming and some do believe in it.*
> > – *Politicians are interested in Global Warming*
> > – *Whatever scientists believes, Global Warming is happening*
>
> Idea #2: *Growing awareness of problems caused by Global Warming*
> > – *People exaggerate climate problems*
> > – *melting ice caps and losing our fresh water supply*
>
> Idea #3: *Problem in food supply*
> > – *Global Warming may change our growing seasons*
> > – *May change the kinds of foods we can grow*

This is the first draft of the paragraph, and many students might just leave it the way it is. However, there are some changes that must be made.

The first question to ask yourself when you are beginning to revise your paragraph is this:
- Is there any part of the paragraph that needs more information? In other words, what must I add to this paragraph to make it better?

>>> Look at Idea #1:
> There are three details, and although they aren't very good, we will leave them there for now.

>>> Look at Idea #2:
> > *Growing awareness of problems caused by Global Warming*
> > – *People exaggerate climate problems*
> > – *Melting ice caps and losing our fresh water supply*
>
> Here there are only two details when there should be three. So, let's add a new idea here.
> > – *Glacier melting will increase the height of oceans and take away inhabited shorelines.*
>
> Now we have three details for Idea #2.

>>> Look at Idea #3:
> > *Problem in food supply*
> > – *Global Warming may change our growing seasons*
> > – *May change the kinds of foods we can grow*

Lesson 6: Editing and Revising **75**

>   Again, we have only included two details for this idea, so let's add another one now.
>   - *Rain is becoming polluted from industry etc. so crops are not getting fresh water.*

We agree at this point that all the details that we have listed are not great. But, adding details so that each idea contains three points is the beginning step for revising your work.

Let's rewrite the paragraph with the new details added.

> There is a great deal of talk today about Global Warming. Scientists are not in agreement about this phenomenon. Some feel that human beings are not responsible for the climate change that we have been experiencing over the past century, whereas other scientists claim that human beings are doing things that are definitely responsible for the warming trend. Politicians are also interested in Global Warming. But whatever scientists tell us we cannot ignore the fact that our climate is changing and we need to look at the reasons for this. In the past few years, there has been a growing awareness of the potential problems caused by Global Warming. People sometimes exaggerate the effects of global warming. Melting the icecaps too quickly can produce flooding, and in time could destroy our access to clean water. **As well, glacier melting will increase the height of oceans and take away inhabited shorelines where people live and play**. One of the great problems of Global Warming involves food supply. Although growing seasons may be increased, there is a danger that the world could change the kinds of foods that we grow now. **In addition, the rain may become more and more polluted from industrial and vehicle discharge that our crops will not get fresh water**. Global Warming is a concern and people must learn what they can do to stop it before it becomes a real problem.

You will notice immediately that the paragraph is much longer than the first one! As well, your reader has more information about each idea that you have expressed.

Let's move on the second step in the ARRRP method of revision.

 **Exercise 1**

Each of the following ideas contains only **two details**. Add a third detail that you would use to prove the idea. Be sure that the idea is appropriate!

Example:
Idea: Friends are very important to us.
Details:
- *You can tell them things that you can't tell anyone else.*
- *You can depend on them for support when you need it.*
- *You always have someone to talk to*

1) Idea: *Exercise is good for you*
   Details:
   - *Builds muscle*
   - *Helps you keep a healthy weight*
   -

2) Idea: *Everyone should read a newspaper every day.*
   Details:
   - *It is important to keep up with the news in the world*
   - *The newspaper provides informative articles on current issues*
   -

3) Idea: *All children should be required to do household chores.*
   Details:
   - *Chores teach children to be responsible for their environment*
   - *Doing chores helps parents*
   -

4) Idea: *Traveling is an excellent education.*
   Details:
   - *Learn about different cultures*
   - *Taste different foods*
   -

5) Idea: *Everyone should have a hobby.*
   Details:
   - *Important to have something to occupy spare time*
   - *Hobbies provide the opportunity to learn a skill*
   -

2. Removing Unnecessary or Irrelevant Ideas

> 앞에 나온 paragraph에는 불필요하거나 관련이 없는 idea들이 있습니다. 그러한 관련없는 idea들이 remove되는 과정을 보여줍니다.

Here is the writing plan for the paragraph that we just wrote. We are going to examine it to see if there is any information in it that is unnecessary or inappropriate for the topic.

<u>Writing Plan</u>

>>> <u>Idea #1</u>: *Scientists are not in agreement*
- *Some scientists do not believe in Global Warming and some do believe in it.*
- *Politicians are interested in Global Warming*
- *Whatever science believes, Global Warming is happening*

The second point is that 'politicians are interested in Global Warming' and the point does not relate to the idea at all. So, we can remove that one.

Now Idea #1 looks like this:

>>> <u>Idea #1</u>: *Scientists are not in agreement*
- *Some scientists do not believe in Global Warming and some do believe in it.*
- *(removed)*
- *Whatever science believes, Global Warming is happening*

Now we only have two ideas here, but we will leave that for now!

>>> <u>Idea #2:</u> *Growing awareness of problems caused by Global Warming*
- *People exaggerate climate problems*
- *Melting ice caps and losing our fresh water supply*
- *Glacier melting will increase the height of oceans and take away inhabited shorelines.*

The topic for Idea #2 is our 'growing awareness of the problems caused by Global Warming'. The first detail 'people exaggerate climate problems' has nothing at all to do with the fact that we are becoming aware of problems. So we can **remove** that detail. The last two details both explain the kinds of problems that are caused by global warming, so they are important to keep!

Now Idea #2 looks like this:

Idea #2: *Growing awareness of problems caused by Global Warming*
- *(removed)*
- *Melting ice caps and losing our fresh water supply*
- *Glacier melting will increase the height of oceans and take away inhabited shorelines.*

Again, we have only two details here, but we will ignore that for now.

>>> Idea #3.

The topic is 'problem is food supply' and each one of the details relates well to that topic. So we can keep all of these!

We have applied the first two steps in the revision process: We have **added** details where they were needed, and we have **removed** details that are not appropriate. Since we removed two details, we should go back now and add two good details. So, let's do that now!

Idea #1: *Scientists are not in agreement*
- *Some scientists do not believe in Global Warming and some do believe in it.*
- **Scientific research has had mixed results so it is hard to be sure what to believe**
- *whatever science believes, Global Warming is happening*

Idea #2: *Growing awareness of problems caused by Global Warming*
- **There are reports of more frequent and violent storms around the world**
- *Melting ice caps and losing our fresh water supply*
- *Glacier melting will increase the height of oceans and take away inhabited shorelines.*

With these added details, our paragraph now looks like this:

There is a great deal of talk today about Global Warming. Scientists are not in agreement about this phenomenon. Some feel that human beings are not responsible for the climate change that we have been experiencing over the past century, whereas other scientists claim that human beings are doing things that are definitely responsible for the warming trend. **The reason for this is the fact**

Lesson 6: Editing and Revising

that scientific research has had mixed results, so it is difficult to know what to believe. But whatever scientists tell us we cannot ignore the fact that our climate is changing and we need to look at the reasons for this. In the past few years, there has been a growing awareness of the potential problems caused by Global Warming. **There are reports of more frequent and violent storms around the world**. Melting the icecaps too quickly can produce flooding, and in time could destroy our access to clean water. As well, glacier melting will increase the height of oceans and take away inhabited shorelines where people live and play. One of the great problems of Global Warming involves food supply. Although growing seasons may be increased, there is a danger that the world could change the kinds of foods that we grow now. In addition, the rain may become more and more polluted from industrial and vehicle discharge that our crops will not get fresh water. Global Warming is a concern and people must learn what they can do to stop it before it becomes a real problem.

You have learned how to do the first two steps of revising your work – adding needed details and removing unnecessary details.

 Exercise 2

Each of the following ideas has three details. One of the details is inappropriate. Cross out the detail that does not relate to the topic.

Example:
Idea: Friends are very important to us.
Details:
   a. You can tell them things that you can't tell anyone else.
   b. You can depend on them for support when you need it.
   c. ~~You can't have too many friends.~~

1) Idea: *Fathers have a lot of jobs.*
   Details:
   a. They earn money for their family.
   b. They like to play golf.
   c. They fix things around the house

2) Idea: *Dogs make good pets.*
   Details:
   a. They are very good with children

       b. *They protect their owners*
       c. *They don't like cats*

3) Idea: *Trees are good for the environment.*
   Details:
       a. *They are good for firewood.*
       b. *They give off oxygen into the air*
       c. *They prevent the earth from moving on steep slopes.*

4) Idea: *Disneyland is a popular vacation place.*
   Details:
       a. *There are many rides for both children and adults*
       b. *Disneyland is in California*
       c. *Children can meet all their favorite characters there*

5) Idea: *Cars are better than trucks.*
   Details:
       a. *Women like to drive cars*
       b. *Cars use less gasoline*
       c. *Cars are more comfortable to ride in*

3. Rewording

> Paragraph의 first draft에서는 완벽한 어휘나 표현보다는 idea를 기술하는 데 주력합니다. First draft를 revise하면서 좀더 적절한 어휘 사용 및 효과적인 표현으로 고쳐나갑니다. 아래의 예는 Rewording의 과정을 보여줍니다.

Read the following paragraph carefully.

I don't like going to the mall. There are too many people there, and the noise is bad. People are rude, and they often walk by you and hit you with their shopping bags and purses. Even the clerks in the stores are often rude. Many just stand behind the counter and talk to other people who work in the store and ignore the customers who need help. Some ask you what you want and if you say you are 'just looking' they walk away and ignore you. I avoid going to the mall. I would rather go without something than go to the mall to shop.

When you write your first draft, you should not worry about choosing the perfect word.

In fact, you should just work at getting your ideas down on paper. Then, in the process of revising your work, you can choose better words and more effective ways of stating ideas.

Let's look closely at this paragraph and see where we can improve the wording.

>>> Sentence #1: *I don't like going to the mall.*
   This is a fairly good topic sentence. It tells the reader the subject (going to the mall) and it also indicates the writer's attitude to her subject. (doesn't like it)

>>> Sentence #2: *There are too many people there, and the noise is bad.*
   This sentence has two ideas in it, and neither one of them is particularly well-stated. Let's look at each one of the ideas.

   There are too many people there.
   We need to make the reader actually visualize the number of people, so let's reword to create a feeling of crowds!

   The place is flooded with hordes of people.
   There is a much stronger visual image in this sentence!

Now let's consider the second idea in the sentence:

   The noise is bad.
   The word 'bad' is not very strong. After all, if there are lots of people around, there are better ways to describe the noise they make! Look at the following:

   The noise is deafening.
   This description of the noise let's the reader **feel** the sound of the crowds.

   Here is the new sentence:

   The place is flooded with hordes of people and the noise is deafening.
   This sentence creates a much stronger picture in the reader's mind.

>>> Sentence #3: *People are rude, and they often walk by you and hit you with their shopping bags and purses.*
   This sentence is fairly good but let's use a stronger verb to help the reader feel the crush of the people around.

> *People are rude and they often <u>push past</u> you and <u>bump</u> you with their shopping bags and purses.*

In this new sentence, we get the feeling that the people are actually pushing you out of the way as they go by, bumping against you with the things they are carrying.

>>> Sentence #4: *Even the clerks in the stores are often rude.*

There is no need to change this sentence because it is a good introduction to the next two sentences which explain the idea further.

>>> Sentences #5 & 6: *Many just stand behind the counter and talk to other people who work in the store and ignore the customers who need help. Some ask you what you want and if you say you are 'just looking' they walk away and ignore you.*

Look at this statement: *Many just stand behind the counter and talk to other people who work in the store*

What do you think the clerks are really doing while they **'talk'** behind the counter? Perhaps they are discussing the new items in the store. Maybe they are laughing about a show they saw on television the night before. Or maybe they are complaining about the boss. Try to imagine what the clerks are talking about, and then reword the sentence to show more detail.

Consider the following possibility:

> *Many just stand behind the counter and gossip with the other people who work in the store.*

By using the verb **'gossip'** we have also indicated the writer's attitude. This writer thinks that clerks are rude, and she would probably think that they were wasting their time gossiping rather than serving customers.

Now let's see if we can find a more concise way of saying 'the other people who work in the store'. Look at the following:

> *Many just stand behind the counter and gossip with **the other workers**.*

The phrase, **'the other workers'** says the same thing but it is more concise.

Sentence # 6 is also an explanation of the rudeness of clerks. So, let's try to combine it with the previous sentence.

Many just stand behind the counter and gossip with the other workers while some ask you what you want and if you say you are 'just looking' they walk away and ignore you.

We have added the word **'while'** to join the ideas together and create a better sentence length.

>>> Sentences #7&8: *I avoid going to the mall. I would rather go without something than go to the mall to shop.*

You can combine sentences #7 and #8 too. Look at the following:

I avoid going to the mall; in fact, I would rather go without something than go to the mall to shop.

Now we have one sentence, but there is still work to be done.

We must **reword** the sentence to get rid of the repetition. There is no need to use the word *'mall'* twice. Look at the following:

I avoid going to the mall; in fact, I would rather go without something than go there to shop.

We have looked very carefully at the original paragraph. Although it may seem like a lot of work, the result is worth it!

Here is the **re-worded** paragraph:

I don't like going to the mall. The place is flooded with hordes of people and the noise is deafening. People are rude and they often push past you and bump you with their shopping bags and purses. Even the clerks in the stores are often rude. Many just stand behind the counter and gossip with the other workers while some ask you what you want and if you say you are 'just looking' they walk away and ignore you. I avoid going to the mall; in fact, I would rather go without something than go there to shop.

Here are some things to remember when you are rewording your writing:

— avoid repetitions of words
— use strong descriptive verbs
— join ideas together to make stronger sentences
— help your reader 'feel' the situation

4. Reordering

> First draft에서는 idea들의 순서보다는 그 idea들을 표현하는 데 주력합니다. First draft를 revise하면서 좀더 적절한 순서로 idea들을 재배치합니다. 아래의 예는 reordering의 과정을 보여줍니다.

When we write down our thoughts for the first time, we don't often worry about putting them in the most effective order. As we have said before, the important thing is to get your ideas down on paper, and then use the revision process to make the changes later.

Here are some examples for re-ordering your writing.

When you are telling a story, you want to tell the events in their natural order. Your reader is able to follow events clearly when they know the correct order of the happenings.

Example:
John went to work at noon. He got up a ten o'clock this morning and had his breakfast.

When you look at the two sentences above, you realize that the first one actually happened after the second one. The times are out of order, and therefore it is confusing. It makes more sense if we say:

John got up at ten o'clock this morning and had his breakfast. He went to work at noon.

When you describe a person or a scene, you need to be careful to direct your reader's eyes around the picture, moving logically from one place to another.

Example:
The bedroom is very large. As you stand at the door, you can see a window on one side of the room. The window looks out into the garden. The bed is on another wall, and beside it is a closet.

In the example, it is difficult for the reader to visualize the picture that the writer is trying to establish. The paragraph requires a better order, with words to indicate the location of each item in relation to the other items in the room.

Look at the **reworded** paragraph below:

The bedroom is very large. As you stand at the door, you can see a window on <u>the left side</u> of *the room. This window looks out into the garden. <u>On the opposite wall</u>, there is a bed, and <u>to the left of the bed</u> is the closet.*

This new paragraph now states **the location** of the items within the room. The reader can visualize the room much more clearly.

5. Proofreading

> Editing and revising의 마지막 step은 spelling과 grammar error를 check하는 proofreading입니다.

When you proofread your work, you are looking for the following:

a. errors in spelling
b. errors in grammar and sentence structure

Look at the following example. Imagine that you have done all the previous steps in the revision process, and now you are looking at the final step – proofreading.

I have always loved going to the movies. Being in a dark theatre for two or three hours. It is very relaxing for me. I enjoy action films as well as comedys. But most of all, I like the kind of dramatic films that make me think.

This short paragraph contains two errors that you should find when you proofread.

1) There is a spelling error – comedys. The correct spelling is 'comedies'.
2) There is also a sentence structure error. 'Being in a dark theatre for two or three hours' is an incomplete sentence; that is, it does not have a main verb. You need to complete the sentence by adding a verb.

Here is one possible correction:

Being in a dark theatre for two or three hours is very relaxing for me.

We have joined the ideas from two sentences together to make one complete sentence. By doing that, we have added a main verb – 'is'.

Writing Exercise

You are going to write **three** paragraphs for the following topics. Each paragraph must be 125-150 words in length. Use the attached paragraph planning sheets to help you plan each paragraph.

Topics:

1) My dream
2) Animals
3) Alternative sources of energy
4) Grandparents
5) Freedom of speech
6) Love
7) My favorite singer

Paragraph Planning Sheet

Topic:

Narrowed Topic:

Controlling Idea:

Topic Sentence:

Ideas to support the topic sentence:

1.

2.

3.

Concluding Idea

Paragraph Planning Sheet

Topic:

Narrowed Topic:

Controlling Idea:

Topic Sentence:

Ideas to support the topic sentence:

1.

2.

3.

Concluding Idea

Paragraph Planning Sheet

Topic:

Narrowed Topic:

Controlling Idea:

Topic Sentence:

Ideas to support the topic sentence:

1.

2.

3.

Concluding Idea

Lesson 7: Effective Sentence Structure

1. Varying Sentence Structure

> 지루하고 반복적인 글을 피하기 위해 꼭 필요한 것은 문장구조를 다양하게 하는 것입니다. 다음 방법으로 다양한 문장구조를 만들어봅니다.

Sentence variety applies to all types of writing. You should try to vary the construction of your sentences. If all your sentences have the same structure, they become repetitive and boring to read.

1-1. Changing the Way to Begin Sentences

> 문장 시작을 주어가 아닌 다른 방법으로 함으로써 문장을 다양하게 만듭니다. 자주 쓰이는 방법으로는 아래 5가지가 있습니다.

Five of the most popular special methods of opening sentences are as follows:

1) Use the **past participle** (과거분사) of a verb. These are verb forms that end in **–ed**. For example, the word worried used on its own is the past participle of the verb worry.

   Example: *Worried that her father was lonely, she visited him every day.*

2) Use the **present participle** (현재분사) of a verb. These are verbs which end in **–ing**. For example, the word singing used on its own is the present participle of the verb sing.

   Example: *Singing softly, the child rocked her doll in its cradle.*

3) Use an **adverb**. These words frequently end in **–ly**. Some examples of adverbs include quickly, slowly, sadly, badly, quietly.

   Example: *Quietly, the boy sneaked up the stairs to avoid waking his parents.*

4) Use the **infinitive form** (부정사) of a verb. An infinitive begins with the word "to" and includes a verb. For example, "to look" is an infinitive.

Example: *To look her best at all times, Janet applies makeup every morning.*

5) Use **prepositional** (전치사) **phrases** to introduce sentences. These are phrases that begin with a preposition and include a noun.

Example: *Before the final exam, Betty had to go around asking for an eraser.*

In this sentence, "*Before the final exam*" is a prepositional phrase.

Exercise 1

Rewrite each of the following pairs of sentences into one sentence using the method indicated. Use the examples above to help you if necessary.

1) Use an adverb to begin the sentence.
   Sandra walked all the way downtown.
   She was very slow.

2) Use an infinitive to begin the sentence.
   The boys tried to play their best at all times.
   They wanted to win the game.

3) Use a prepositional phrase to begin the sentence.
   The referee made several bad calls.
   He did this during the basketball game.

4) Use a past participle to begin the sentence.
   The stores in the mall were noisy and hot.
   They were crowded with Christmas shoppers.

5) Use a present participle to begin the sentence.
   Bob managed to catch five large fish.
   He fished for only an hour.

1-2. Use of Semi-Colon

> Semi-Colon을 사용하여 보다 길고 흥미로운 문장으로 만들어 봅니다. Semi-Colon을 쓰는 방법은 3가지가 있습니다.

There are many types of punctuation in writing, but one of the most important to learn about is the semi-colon. Using a semi-colon effectively will help you to write longer, more interesting sentences.

Here are **three** uses of a semi-colon:

1) Combine Two Complete Thoughts

A semi-colon can be used to separate two **complete thoughts** within the same sentence. These two thoughts must be related. In this situation, the semi-colon is functioning as a period inside the sentence.

◎ *Shakespeare wrote a number of tragedies.*
◎ *He also wrote many comedies.*

Here are two sentences which are related to each other. Shakespeare wrote both types of plays. Because the ideas are related, we can put them into the same sentence.

◎ *Shakespeare wrote a number of tragedies; he also wrote many comedies.*

Notice that we have separated the two ideas with a semi-colon. This is only possible to do if the idea in front of the semi-colon and the idea after the semi-colon are complete sentences.

Here is another example:
◎ *Bob is going to the dentist this morning.*
◎ *He has a broken tooth.*

We can join these two ideas together because they are related to each other. Look at how the two ideas can be put into one sentence:

◎ *Bob is going to the dentist this morning; he has a broken tooth*

Again, we are joining the two complete sentences by using a semi-colon.

By putting two or more ideas into one sentence, you can write longer, more interesting sentences.

2) Use with Joining Adverbs

A semi-colon can be used with certain adverbs in sentences. When you use an adverb to join two ideas together, there must be a semi-colon before the adverb and a comma after it. Not all adverbs need this punctuation! You use this punctuation only when an adverb is used to join two ideas together.

Here are two sentences:
- *I am not going to run in the marathon.*
- *I am willing to help out at the checkpoints along the route.*

If we want to put these two ideas into one sentence, we can add an adverb that will join them.
- *I am not going to run in the marathon;* **however***, I am willing to help out at the checkpoints along the route.*

Notice that we have added a semi-colon before the adverb 'however' and a comma after the adverb.

Here are some more examples:

Two sentences:
I lost my wallet.
I don't have any identification with me.

Adding a joining adverb:
I lost my wallet; **consequently***, I don't have any identification with me.*

Two sentences:
I enjoy making dinner for large groups.
I often have dinner parties in my home.

Adding a joining adverb:
I enjoy making dinner for large groups; **therefore***, I often have dinner parties in my home.*

The most common joining adverbs are:

however,	moreover,	therefore,	in addition,
subsequently,	consequently,	additionally,	instead,

It is possible to join ideas in many different ways. Sometimes it is more effective to use just the semi-colon to join the two ideas, and sometimes it is more effective to use an adverb to join the two ideas. The writer needs to choose the method that works the best for a particular situation.

Example:
Two Sentences:
I have had the flu this week.
I haven't been able to go to the office.

Using just the semi-colon:
I have had the flu this week; I haven't been able to get to the office.

Using an adverb:
I have had the flu this week; consequently, I haven't been able to get to the office.

Use as a "Super-Comma"

Lastly, the semi-colon is used as a "super-comma" to separate a series of phrases or clauses that are very long or have punctuation like commas within them.

Example:
The members of the committee included: Joe Brown, a student at the university; Mike Patten, the vice-president of the class; and Kim Edwards, a professor.

You will note that each item in the list contains a comma, and the items in the list are separated by semi-colons.

 **Exercise 2**

Combine each of the following sentences in two ways:
    a. Using only a semi-colon
    b. Using a joining adverb

I love to grow things. I have a big garden every summer.

Semi-colon:

Adverb:

Mona is not feeling well. She is sleeping a lot during the day.

    Semi-colon:

    Adverb:

My brother had a car accident last week. He is going to buy a new vehicle soon.

    Semi-colon:

    Adverb:

Our cat ran away last week. She came back this morning.

    Semi-colon:

    Adverb:

The aircraft that we were riding in had very hard seats. We were very uncomfortable for the whole trip.

    Semi-colon:

    Adverb:

Exercise 3

Put semi-colons in the correct places in the following sentences.

1) Our class includes the following successful people: John Dean, president of Yale University Anne Fortune, chairperson of Auto Canada and Virginia Dole, Minister of Finance for Alberta.

2) The Art Gallery of Scotch Creek is pleased to display the following paintings: 'Echo', by John O'Toole 'Treescape', by Marion McVeen 'Foolishness', by Andrew Carter and 'England', by Annette Andrews.

Avoid Using a Comma When a Semicolon is Needed:

Incorrect: *The cow is brown, it is also old.*
Correct: *The cow is brown; it is also old.*

Both parts of the sentence are independent clauses, and commas should not be used to connect independent clauses. This mistake is known as a comma splice.

Incorrect: *I like cows, however, I hate the way they smell.*
Correct: *I like cows; however, I hate the way they smell.*

Avoid Using a Semicolon When a Comma is Needed:

Incorrect: *The cow is brown; but not old.*
Correct: *The cow is brown, but not old.*

The coordinating conjunction 'but' doesn't require a semicolon, **since the second part of the sentence isn't an independent clause**. Don't use the semi-colon with coordinate conjunctions like "and", "but", "for", "so" and "yet".

Incorrect: *Because cows smell; they offend me.*
Correct: *Because cows smell, they offend me*

The first part is **not** an independent clause, so no semicolon is required.

Exercise 4

Rewrite the following sentences making the necessary corrections in comma and semi-colon use.

1) Jim and John are going to California this week however they are not going to Disneyland.

2) I have a very sore throat I am going to see the doctor this afternoon.

3) Ginny is not going to the party tonight instead she is staying home to look after her little sister.

4) I want to learn to write well consequently I must learn grammar.

5) I am very hungry I am going to make something to eat.

2. Sentence Combining

> 계속해서 Sentence Combining을 공부합니다. Writing이 익숙하지 못한 학생들에게 흔히 나타나는 문제점은 짧고 단순한 문장의 나열입니다. Sentence Combing은 단순한 문장들을 연결하여 힘있고 흥미로운 문장을 만드는 중요한 writing 기법입니다.

"Sentence Combining" is an important skill to help you avoid choppy sentences in your writing and create longer, more interesting sentences. Choppy sentences are those that are very short and uninteresting.

There are many ways to put ideas together into sentences, and the exercises that you do in this lesson are designed to give you the opportunity to develop your own unique writing style.

> Sentence Combing 하는 방법은 여러가지가 있습니다. 아래는 3개의 단순한 문장들이 어떻게 하나의 문장으로 combine 되는지 5가지 예를 보여줍니다.

Example
- *Learning grammar helps you to write correctly.*
- *It helps you to understand the structure of a language.*
- *Researchers tell us that this is true.*

Five examples to combine these sentences are as follows:

  a. *Learning grammar helps you to write correctly and to understand the structure of a language, according to researchers.*
  b. *Besides helping to write correctly, learning grammar also helps you to understand the structure of a language, according to researchers.*
  c. *According to researchers, learning grammar helps you to write correctly; in addition, it helps you to understand the structure of a language.*
  d. *Not only does learning grammar help you to write correctly, it also helps you to understand the structure of a language, according to researchers.*

> e. Researchers say that writing correctly and understanding the structure of language are the result of learning grammar.

There are many possibilities for constructing a sentence from the three ideas. The way you choose to combine the ideas will be in keeping with your own unique writing style.

> 다양하게 Sentence Combing하는 방법을 공부합니다. Writing을 할 때에는 문장의 다양성이 중요하므로 한 가지 방법보다 모든 방법에 익숙해 지도록 하세요.

It is important to have variety in the structure of your sentences. As you combine ideas, think about the following:

2-1. Create Compound Sentences

> 등위접속사 (and, but, or, so)로 compound sentence (중문)을 만들어 문장을 combine 합니다. Compound sentence에서는 문장의 모든 idea들이 같은 중요도를 가집니다.

When you have two or more complete thoughts that are related, they can become parts of the same sentence. To do this, you must add **coordinate conjunctions** (등위접속사: and, but, or, nor, so). The process of joining these ideas together is called "coordination" and the result is a **compound sentence**.

Look at the following examples:
  Original: *Dan tried to climb the ladder to the roof. The ladder collapsed. Dan fell.*
  Compound: *Dan tried to climb the ladder to the roof, <u>but</u> the ladder collapsed <u>and</u> Dan fell.*

In the compound sentence, the writer has included all three ideas in one sentence. With the use of coordinate conjunctions, the writer has indicated that all the ideas are of equal importance in the sentence.

 Exercise 5

Rewrite each of the following sets of sentences using appropriate coordinating conjunctions.

1) The dog wouldn't come when it was called.
   The owner put him on a leash.

2) My friend went looking for a job yesterday.
   She found a job at the local supermarket.

3) Our cat really enjoys being outdoors.
   She likes to sit by the fireplace in the evening.

4) My father really loves to read.
   He has read so many books that it is difficult to find one that he hasn't read.

2-2. Create Complex Sentences

> Main clause (주절)과 Subordinate clause (종속절)로 이루어진 Complex Sentence (복문)으로 문장을 combine 해봅니다. Complex Sentence에서는 Main Clause가 Subordinate Clause 보다 더 중요한 idea를 포함합니다.

Another way of combining sentences is to add a subordinate conjunction.

When you have two or more ideas, you need to decide which idea is to be the main one. Then, you need to add **subordinate conjunctions** (종속접속사) to subordinate the other ideas in the sentence. Remember that the main idea (main clause) can stand alone as a sentence; however, the subordinate ideas (dependent clauses) depend on the main one and cannot stand on their own as sentences.

The following are subordinate conjunctions:

after	if, even if	when, whenever
although, though	in order that	where, wherever
as	since	whether
because	that, so that	which, whichever
before	unless	while
even though	until	who
how	what, whatever	whose

Look at the following complex sentence:
   Although I wanted to go to the movie, I stayed home to complete a difficult assignment.

The main idea (the idea that the writer wanted to emphasize) is: I stayed home to *complete a difficult assignment.* This idea is expressed in the form of a complete sentence and thus can stand alone. The less important idea – Although I wanted to go to the movie – is the dependent or subordinate clause. Because the sentence contains a subordinate clause, it is called a **complex sentence**.

Here is another example of a complex sentence:
Because he was such a good athlete, his coach named him the most valuable player on the team.

In this example, as in the first example, the subordinate clause is at the beginning of the sentence. When this happens, you must add a comma after the subordinate clause.

Here is another example of a complex sentence:
I say my prayers before I go to sleep at night.

This time, the main clause *(I say my prayers)* comes at the beginning of the sentence and there is no need for a comma to separate it from the dependent clause *(before I go to sleep at night)*.

Exercise 6

Join the following pairs of sentences together using appropriate subordinating conjunctions.

Example:
The dog barked when it was left outside.
The owner decided to keep it in the house.
Because the dog barked when it was left outside, the owner decided to keep it in the house.

1) I had a toothache.
   I went to the dentist.

2) The man sat down on the chair.
   The chair broke.

3) Our old car broke down for the third time.
   We decided to buy a new one.

2–3 Placing Adjectives or Verbs in a Series

> 형용사 또는 동사를 한 문장 안에서 연결함으로써 간결하고 세련된 문장을 만듭니다.

Sometimes it is possible to put adjectives together to avoid choppy sentences. Look at the following example:

Original: *I have a new car. It is shiny and red.*
Revised: *I have a new, shiny, red car.*

You can do the same kind of thing with verbs. Look at the following:

Original: *The child fell off his bike. He grazed his knees. He broke his arm.*
Revised: *The child fell off his bike, grazed his knees, and broke his arm.*

 **Exercise 7**

Write each of the following sets of sentences as a single sentence, making any necessary corrections to the wording. Be sure to add commas where necessary. Use the sentences above as examples.

1) The dog ran out of the yard.
   It ran down the street.
   It ran into the store.

2) The cafeteria served food.
   The cafeteria was noisy.
   The food was greasy.
   The cafeteria was crowded.
   The food was cold.

3) By midnight, I had finished my essay.
   I had edited it carefully.
   I had typed it up on the computer.
   I had printed it out to hand in the next day.

4) The bear sat on the log.
   The bear was fat.
   The log was rotten.
   The bear was old.

5) The doctor took the man's temperature.
   The doctor was young.
   The patient was old.
   The doctor was inexperienced.
   The patient was miserable.

2-4 Use Modifiers in Different Ways

> Modifiers (수식어)의 위치를 변화시켜 봅니다.

Sentences to be combined:
> Don is an excellent baseball player.
> He gets very nervous when he plays.
> He rubs his hat for good luck.

Combination #1:
> Don is an excellent baseball player who gets <u>nervous</u> before every game and rubs his hat for good luck.
> (In this combination, the writer has left all the modifiers in the same order as the original.)

Combination #2:
> Don is an excellent but very <u>nervous</u> baseball player who rubs his hat for good luck.
> (Here the writer has moved the adjective 'nervous' and created a more interesting combination of ideas.)

Combining ideas in your own way is important for you in developing your personal writing style. There are many ways to combine ideas, and the way you choose is an indication of the relationship you see between ideas. Learning how to combine ideas in several different ways allows you to broaden your approach and strengthen your writing style.

 **Exercise 8**

Combine each of the following groups of sentences into one strong statement.
- You must combine each group in <u>two</u> different ways.
- Be creative! Use different combining methods for each group!

1)
- *Television Reality shows are very popular today.*
- *They deal with so-called life situations.*

   Combining #1

   Combining #2

2)
- *Rock and Roll developed during the 1950's and 1960's.*
- *One of the earliest Rock and Roll artists was Elvis Presley.*
- *Buddy Holly also made Rock and Roll popular with the teens of that age.*

   Combining #1

   Combining #2

3)
- *There have been many inventions in the past one hundred years.*
- *The telephone, the television, the car, and the computer are major technological advances in that time.*
- *People who were born in the 1920's have seen an amazing number of advancements.*

   Combining #1

Combining #2

4)
- *Jean is a really good student.*
- *Jean does especially well in English.*
- *She also is a good science student.*

Combining #1

Combining #2

 **Exercise 9**

1) This passage is very choppy. Re-write the paragraph combining ideas to create **three** longer, more interesting sentences. Include all the ideas, but don't add any new ones!

   My name is Sam. I am an immigrant from France. I am finding it hard to adapt to my new country. I can't speak English. Most of my friends can't speak French. I miss my friends from my hometown near Paris. I like Canada. I want to learn to be happy here.

   Write your paragraph here:

2) The following paragraph contains many short sentences. Combine the sentences in the paragraph. Create **two** strong sentences. Make sure that each sentence begins differently.

Christmas dinner is always special. We have lots of traditional foods. We eat turkey, dressing, vegetables and potatoes. We have pies for dessert. Usually we have apple and mince pie. We also have shortbread. We always eat too much at Christmas dinner.

Write your paragraph here:

3) Rewrite the following paragraph combining sentences to make the writing stronger and more interesting. You must create four sentences. You may change the wording to make the sentences flow nicely.

I love rainy days if they don't come too often. I love the sound of a gentle rain. I stay inside and find interesting things to do. I watch television. I like to read books. I play computer games. I even have a nap whenever I want. However, I like sunny days too.

Write your paragraph here:

✎ Writing Exercise

You are going to write **three** paragraphs for the following topics. Each paragraph must be 125-150 words in length. Use the attached paragraph planning sheets to help you plan each paragraph.

Topics:

1. The best day in my school career.
2. What I have learned from experience.
3. Honesty
4. My dream car
5. Food I love (or hate)
6. Self-Esteem
7. The best (worst) vacation my family ever experienced.

Paragraph Planning Sheet

Topic:

Narrowed Topic:

Controlling Idea:

Topic Sentence:

Ideas to support the topic sentence:

1.

2.

3.

Concluding Idea

Paragraph Planning Sheet

Topic:

Narrowed Topic:

Controlling Idea:

Topic Sentence:

Ideas to support the topic sentence:

1.

2.

3.

Concluding Idea

Paragraph Planning Sheet

Topic:

Narrowed Topic:

Controlling Idea:

Topic Sentence:

Ideas to support the topic sentence:

1.

2.

3.

Concluding Idea

Lesson 8: Use of Effective Language

1. Use of Descriptive Adjectives

> 학생들이 흔히 쓰는 형용사는 막연하고 모호한 표현일 경우가 많습니다. 아래 예에서 보는 바와 같이 'nice'라는 형용사는 많은 뜻을 함축하고 있어 sentence가 나타내고자 하는 바를 제대로 표현하지 못합니다. 좀더 구체적인 형용사를 사용하면 문장의 뜻을 보다 효과적이고 생생하게 나타낼 수 있습니다.

An adjective is a word which describes a noun. Although adjectives are not necessary in sentences, they help to make things clearer for the reader.

Some adjectives are not very descriptive. Look at the following examples:

*It is a **nice** day today.*

The word **nice** is an adjective to describe the word day. However, what does it really tell us about the type of day? Not very much! In fact, what is a nice day? Is the weather good? Did something nice happen? We need more detail to understand the meaning of the sentence.

Each reader has a different idea of the word nice. For one person, it might mean that a cool autumn day is nice. For another, it might mean that a warm summer day is nice.

We might replace the adjective nice by using different adjectives that are more descriptive. Look at the following examples:

*It is a **sunny** day today.*
*It is a **warm** day today.*
*It is a **warm**, sunny day today.*

The three sentences above explain to the reader what kind of day it is: sunny and warm. The reader now knows what the writer means by the word **nice**.

 **Exercise 1**

Replace each of the boldface adjectives with one or two more descriptive adjectives. Rewrite the sentence in the space provided.

Example:
*Original sentence: The garden had many varieties of **beautiful** flowers.*
*New sentence: The garden had many varieties of **colorful, fragrant** flowers.*

Now the reader knows that the garden was **beautiful** because the flowers had lots of ***color*** and ***smelled sweet.***

Here is another example:
*Original sentence: The water was very **nice** today.*
*New sentence: The water was very **calm** today.*

There may have been many reasons why the water was nice. But this writer meant that it was nice because it was calm.

Now it's your turn! Ask yourself what you mean by the word in boldface. Then choose an adjective (or two) to explain your meaning. (Use a dictionary or thesaurus if needed.)

1) We had a **lovely** vacation in Paris.
New sentence:

2) The girl in the commercial was very **pretty**.
New sentence:

3) The woman had a very **old** face.
New sentence:

4) Every morning I wake up and look into the mirror. My face always looks bad.
New sentence:

5) I read a **good** book last week.
New sentence:

6) The coffee that she made was not **nice**.
New sentence:

7) We had an **interesting** experience at the zoo.
   New sentence:

8) What a **super** father he is!
   New sentence:

Descriptive Adjectives

Appearance		
Adorable	Filthy	Smiling
Attractive	Gentle	Splendid
Alluring	Glamorous	Self-assured
Beautiful	Handsome	Snobbish
Bewildered	Homely	Thoughtful
Confident	Hurt	Tense
Cheerful	Ill-mannered	Timid
Cultured	Jolly	Upset
Clumsy	Kind-hearted	Vivacious
Drab	Lovely	Wonderful
Dull	Magnificent	Worried
Dynamic	Nervous	Wild
Disillusioned	Pleasant	Zaftig
Elegant	Perfect	
Fair	Plucky	

Personality		
Aggressive	Fearless	Successful
Ambitious	Generous	Sedate
Amused	Gifted	Sincere
Brave	Helpful	Selfish
Bright	Harmonious	Talented
Cruel	Hesitant	Thrifty
Combative	Instinctive	Truculent
Co-operative	Jealous	Unbiased
Cowardly	Knowledgeable	Voracious

Dangerous	Loner	Witty
Diligent	Mysterious	Wise
Determined	Naughty	Warm
Disagreeable	Pleasing	Zany
Evil	Placid	
Frank	Punctual	

Feelings		
Afraid	Fine	Sorrowful
Angry	Good	Silly
Anxious	Grieving	Somber
Bad	Horrible	Sore
Bored	Happy	Tired
Calm	Hungry	Troubled
Confused	Ill	Testy
Comfortable	Jovial	Unwell
Creepy	Kind	Vengeful
Depressed	Lively	Wicked
Disturbed	Mature	Weary
Dominating	Nice	Wrong
Deceitful	Proud	Zestful
Envious	Peaceful	
Faithful	Protective	

Shape		
Broad	Flat	Square
Crooked	Hollow	Skinny
Circular	Narrow	Steep
Distorted	Round	Wide

Size		
Big	Huge	Petite
Colossal	Large	Tall
Great	Miniature	Thin
Gigantic	Mammoth	Tiny

Time		
Ancient	Fast	Rapid
Annual	Late	Swift
Brief	Modern	Slow
Early	Old	Young

Quantity		
Abundant	Extra	Many
Bountiful	Few	Multiple
Cumbersome	Heavy	Numerous
Empty	Myriad	Substantial

Sound		
Blaring	Melancholic	Squeaking
Cooing	Noisy	Silent
Deafening	Soft	Thundering
Loud	Shrill	Whispering

Taste		
Bitter	Icy	Sour
Delicious	Juicy	Salty
Fresh	Spicy	Tasty
Hot	Sweet	Tasteless

Touch		
Hard	Slippery	Soft
Loose	Sticky	Tender
Rough	Sharp	Uneven
Smooth	Scattered	Wet

Color		
Azure	Crimson	Magenta
Aqua	Cyan	Orange
Blue	Gold	Pink
Black	Green	Turquoise

2. Use of Descriptive Verbs

> 형용사의 경우와 같이 동사도 행동을 묘사할 수 있습니다. 아래의 예는 Descriptive Verb를 사용하여 문장의 뜻을 보다 효과적이고 생생하게 나타내는 것을 보여줍니다.

A **verb** is a word which describes an action. Although we tend to think that 'adjectives' are the only descriptive words, 'verbs' can also be very descriptive. In fact, in most languages, there are many verbs that describe the same kind of action. Look at the following:

*John **goes** down the street to school.*

The verb 'go' is a perfectly acceptable verb to describe how John gets to school. However, if we look more closely at John as he 'goes' down the street, we might notice something about the **way** he goes.

*John **runs** down the street to the school.*
*John **skips** down the street to school.* (skip: 깡충 뛰다, 가볍게 뛰다)
*John **leaps** down the street to school.* (leap: 도약하다, 뛰어오르다)
*John **jogs** down the street to school.* (jog: 조깅하다)

In each of the sentences above, John's action is different yet each one describes how John 'goes' down to the school. And in each sentence, the way John moves is more descriptive than simply saying he 'goes' down the street to school.

 **Exercise 2**

Here are some ordinary verbs in sentences. Think of more descriptive verbs that would fit appropriately into the sentences. Write the sentence again for each new verb. (Use a dictionary or thesaurus if needed.)

1) The girls **were talking** at the lunch table.

2) The two boys **laughed** when the teacher walked by their desks.

3) The dog **jumped** into the water.

4) I **saw** the accident and I **told** the police.

3. Use of Active and Passive Voice

> 습관적으로 Passive Voice(수동태) 문장을 즐겨 쓰는학생이 많습니다. Active Voice(능동태)와 Passive Voices는 문장에서 행위의 주체를 강조하는지 또는 행위의 대상을 강조하는 지에 따라 결정되어야 합니다. 그러나 Essay에서는 꼭 필요한 경우를 제외하고 주로 Active Voice를 사용해야 합니다.

In this lesson, we are going to talk about **active** and **passive voice**.

In order to make the most effective use of sentences, we have to decide which parts of the sentence are to be emphasized. One way that we can do this is to make the best use of active and passive voices.

Students often use the passive voice in their writing when it is not appropriate.

We use the active voice in sentences when the person or thing doing the action is more important than the receiver of the action.

You use the passive voice when you want to focus the attention of the sentence on the person or thing that is affected by the action.

The active voice is the strongest method of presenting ideas in your writing because it leads the reader in a natural order from subject to verb to object. The passive voice leaves the doer of the action until the end of the sentence, and often the impact of the idea is lost by then. Use the passive voice very sparingly in your writing!

When you write essays, you should use the active voice whenever possible. In general, active verbs are more effective than passive ones because they give your writing a simpler and stronger style.

The passive voice is often used in business, because the object of an action is often more important than those who perform the action.

Look at this example:
  ◎ *Our employees have produced over 10,000 new cars this week.*

This sentence is in the active voice where the verb tells us what the subject did.

In this sentence, the emphasis is on 'our employees' because that is the subject of the sentence, but is that really the important point in the sentence? Is it important that the 'employees' produced the new cars? Or, in this case, is it more important that 10,000 new cars were produced?

If this was part of a report to the owners of the car company, the owners would probably be more interested in the number of cars being produced. They know that the employees produce them. So the report might say this:
- ◎ *10,000 new cars were produced by our employees this week.*

Now the sentence is in the passive voice and we learn what happened to the subject.

Here is another example:

If you want to emphasize the author's name, you would use the active voice.
- ◎ *William Shakespeare wrote 'Hamlet'.*

However, if you want to emphasize the play, you would write it in the passive voice.
- ◎ *'Hamlet' was written by William Shakespeare.*

The writer must decide which element of the sentence he or she wishes to emphasize for the reader.

Although the passive voice is effective in writing reports, it is not generally recommended for use in essays. Often students feel that the passive voice sounds better. They seem to think that using the passive voice makes them sound more intelligent. But the effect is just the opposite! When you write a paragraph or an essay, you are trying to create the most dynamic approach possible. You want to get you ideas out in the strongest manner possible.

4. Parallel Structure

> 문장 내에서는 모든 표현이 Parallel Structure (병렬구조)를 가져야 합니다. 즉, 한 문장 내의 word, phrases 그리고 clauses는 문법적으로 같은 구조를 가져야 합니다.

In this lesson, you will learn about parallel structure. When there is a list of words or phrases (two words/phrases or more) in a sentence, the words must all be grammatically same. This "sameness" is called parallel structure.

Parallel structure must exist with single words, short phrases, and even clauses contained in the same sentence. Usually parallel structures are joined by using co-ordinate conjunctions. (and, or, nor).

Structure that isn't parallel sometimes isn't precisely grammatically wrong, but it comes across as awkward. Parallelism has long been a technique used in writing.

Parallel structure helps to organize ideas, making a text or speech easier to understand. Parallel structure can also create a satisfying rhythm in the language an author uses.

4-1. Parallel Structure with Words

> 문장에서 단어 사용시 문법적으로 동일한 형태를 취해야 합니다. 즉, 형용사는 형용사로, 부사는 부사로, 과거형은 과거형으로 일관성을 유지하여야 합니다.

Here is an example:

Incorrect: *The student was asked to write his report **quickly, accurately, and so it was clear**.*

Correct: *The student was asked to write his report **quickly, accurately, and clearly**.*

In the incorrect sentence, the first two items are adverbs and the last item is not. We have corrected the sentence so that all the words are now adverbs and thus the sentence has parallel structure.

Here is another example:

Incorrect: *My mother is **beautiful, sensitive** and **knows a lot**.*

Correct: *My mother is **beautiful, sensitive** and **knowledgeable**.*

In the incorrect sentence, the writer has used two adjectives to describe her mother.

However the third characteristic of the mother is not listed as an adjective. To get parallel structure, we have re-written the sentence to include all the items as adjectives.

Here is another example:
Incorrect: *His mother told him that he would be successful because he **listened** to the teacher, **followed** instructions and was always doing his homework well.*

Correct: *His mother told him that he would be successful because he **listened** to the teacher, **followed** instructions and **did** his homework well.*

In the incorrect sentence, the writer has used the past tense of the verbs listened and followed. However, the writer has used a present form of the verb doing. In order to create parallel structure in the sentence, the writer must find a way to put the word 'doing' into the past tense to match the other verbs. The corrected sentence shows you how he did that.

4-2. Parallel Structure with Infinitive Phrases

> 문장내에서 to-부정사는 to-부정사로, 동명사(-ing)는 동명사로 일관성을 유지합니다.

The infinitive of a verb takes the following form:
- **to** swim
- **to** dance
- **to** see

As you see, the infinitive of a verb has the word 'to' in front of it.

Now, look at how infinitive phrases must be used together in sentences so that there is **parallel structure**.

Example:
Incorrect: *I like **to ski, to swim**, and **riding** a bike.*
Correct: *I like **to ski**, to swim and **to ride** a bike.*

In the incorrect sentence, the first two items, 'to ski' and 'to swim' are infinitives, but the last item, 'riding' is not. To give this sentence parallel structure, we must change the last item to match the first two. That means, we have to make 'riding' into its infinitive form, 'to ride'.

4-3. Parallel Structure with Clauses

> 문장내에서 clause들도 문법적으로 같은 형태를 취해야 합니다.

If you begin to write a series of clauses, you must complete the sentence with clauses. Look at the following examples:

> Incorrect: *The teacher told the students **that they should get** a good night's sleep, that **they should eat** a good breakfast, and to relax before writing the test.*

> Correct: *The teacher told the students **that they should get** a good night's sleep, **that they should eat** a good breakfast, and that **they should relax** before writing the test.*

You can see the difference in the two sentences. In the incorrect sentence, the writer has changed the structure of the clauses in the sentence. He has written three items:

- **that they should get** a good night's sleep
- **that they should eat** a good breakfast
- **to relax** before writing the test.

The third item is not parallel. It is not written in the same form as the first two. You can see that the problem has been fixed in the correct sentence. Now the items look like this:

- **that they should get** a good night's sleep
- **that they should eat** a good breakfast
- **that they should relax** before writing the test.

All the clauses are structured in the same way.

 Exercise 3

Rewrite each of the following sentences to correct the problems with the parallel structure.

1) Careful campers remember to put out their fires, leaving the campsite clean, and to remove all their garbage.

2) The waiter at the restaurant reminded us that we should order quickly, eat slowly and to tip him well.

3) You will be responsible for planning the party, to buy the food, and cleaning the room.

4) The hardware store sells hand tools, home appliances and materials for building.

5) In order to become an actress, Anne is taking drama lessons, working for a theatre company, and auditions for roles.

6) At the beauty salon, I had my hair washed, dried and color was added.

7) Many people like to go on vacation, spending money, and to sleep late in the morning.

8) To be a good role model you should consider your behavior, your relationships with others and what you look like when you go out in public.

9) Modern appliances will help you to do the laundry, cooking food and wash dirty dishes.

10) Mike likes movies that are suspenseful, interesting and filled with excitement.

Writing Exercise

You are going to write **three** paragraphs for the following topics. Each paragraph must be 125-150 words in length. Use the attached paragraph planning sheets to help you plan each paragraph.

Topics

1. My favorite story about my family.

2. A time that I would prefer to forget.

3. The best thing I have ever done.

4. Something that makes you feel sad

5. The best birthday present you ever received

6. Courage

Paragraph Planning Sheet

Topic:

Narrowed Topic:

Controlling Idea:

Topic Sentence:

Ideas to support the topic sentence:

1.

2.

3.

Concluding Idea

Paragraph Planning Sheet

Topic:

Narrowed Topic:

Controlling Idea:

Topic Sentence:

Ideas to support the topic sentence:

1.

2.

3.

Concluding Idea

Paragraph Planning Sheet

Topic:

Narrowed Topic:

Controlling Idea:

Topic Sentence:

Ideas to support the topic sentence:

1.

2.

3.

Concluding Idea

Part II*

Writing an Essay

Lesson 9: Structure of an Essay

> 이번 lesson부터는 Essay를 공부합니다. Essay는 흔히 5개의 paragraph로 구성됩니다. 아래에서 보는 바와 같이 introduction (서론), body (본론) 그리고 conclusion (결론)으로 구성됩니다.

An essay is a piece of writing that expresses the author's opinion on a subject. The author's opinion can be developed through several types of essays. But in all cases, the end result must effectively convince the reader that the author's opinion has value.

In the essay lesson, you will learn to write five-paragraph essays. Why write essays of this length? A five-paragraph essay allows the writer to develop three strong points to prove his/her opinion. An essay with fewer paragraphs is less convincing.

Look at the following diagram. It will help you understand the structure of a five-paragraph essay. Each box represents one paragraph in the essay.

Introductory Paragraph

Body Paragraph 1

Body Paragraph 2

Body Paragraph 3

Concluding Paragraph

Let's look at what is contained in each section of the essay.

1. Introductory Paragraph

> Introductory Paragraph (서론)은 Hook, Thesis, Blueprint로 구성됩니다.

There are three things that are included in the introductory paragraph of an essay.

a. Hook

> Hook은 한두 문장으로 구성되며 독자의 흥미를 이끌어내는 역할을 합니다. Hook을 쓰는 방법은 Lesson 11에서 다시 자세히 공부할 것입니다.

The essay needs to begin with a sentence or two about the subject of the essay. These sentences should be interesting enough to make the reader want to read on. This is called the "**hook**". This section of the essay **hooks** the reader's interest, the same way that a fisherman **hooks** a fish.

b. Thesis

> Thesis는 essay에서 가장 중요한 부분이며 essay에서 논하고자 하는 주제입니다. Thesis에 대해서는 Lesson 10에서 자세히 공부할 것입니다.

The hook should lead naturally into the thesis of the essay. Here in a sentence (or maybe two) the writer introduces the topic that is going to be proved in the essay. It will also indicate the author's opinion about the topic. **The thesis is the most important part of your essay**, since it will direct the course of the entire essay. We will be doing a lot of work on making your thesis writing strong and forceful!

c. Blueprint

> Blueprint에서는 essay의 전개하고자 하는 내용을 소개합니다. 즉, Essay의 주제인 thesis를 뒷받침하는 main idea들을 Blueprint에서 요약해서 보여줍니다.

The third part of the introductory paragraph is a blueprint which mentions the three **main ideas** which the author will use to prove his/her opinion. It is important to state the ideas in the same order as you intend to discuss them in the essay.

2. Body Paragraphs

> Body (본론) 부분은 introduction의 blueprint에서 소개된 main idea들을 각각 설명하고 전개합니다. Thesis를 충분히 prove하기 위해서는 통상 3개의 body paragraph를 필요로 합니다. 그러나 그 이상 또는 이하인 경우도 상황에 따라 가능합니다.

Each of the body paragraphs of the essay will develop **one** of the **main ideas** introduced in the blueprint of the introductory paragraph. The ideas are developed by different methods, but in each case, the writer will use at least **three** well-explained supporting details to prove each idea. It is also important to conclude each body paragraph with a sentence that pulls the whole paragraph together, or makes a comment on what you have been saying.

You know that it is important to have a strong, clear thesis. You can't prove something if you don't know exactly what it is you are talking about!

Then you need to have three good topic sentences, one for each of the three body paragraphs in your essay.

Now your job is to develop the topic sentences into interesting, informative paragraphs.

You need to remember some of the rules for writing good paragraphs. There is nothing new here! Just like any other paragraph you have ever written, the sentences in the body paragraphs of an essay must be related to and support the topic sentence of the paragraph.

Like other paragraphs, you can generate details in any of the following ways:

- Give examples.
- Show how certain things are similar.
- Show how things are different from one another.
- Tell a story to illustrate your point.
- Explain a difficult idea or give a definition.
- Discuss the cause and effect of certain things.
- Answer questions you think your reader might have.

If all the sentences in the paragraph support the topic sentence and the topic sentence supports the main thesis, then your essay will have unity.

3. Conclusion

> Conclusion (결론)에서는 서론에서 언급한 thesis와 blueprint를 다시 한번 restate 하면서 독자를 설득합니다. 그러나 서론의 단순 반복이거나 essay의 요약이어서는 안됩니다. Conclusion 쓰는 법에 대해서는 Lesson 11에서 다시 자세히 배울것 입니다.

The concluding paragraph briefly restates the thesis and, at times, can refer to the main ideas made in the essay. However, the concluding paragraph should not be simply a summary of the essay. It can be used effectively to persuade the reader to think about what you have said, but it should not introduce any new ideas about the topic. The writer can use the concluding paragraph to present a final thought about the subject she/he has chosen.

Basically, the conclusion should remind the reader of the thesis and restate the blueprint in a different way. Simply repeating your introduction is not an acceptable concluding paragraph. You will learn a number of ways to write a concluding paragraph; however, to begin with, you will use a basic method to familiarize yourself with the concept of a conclusion.

Example of a Five-Paragraph Essay

> 아래는 좋지 않은 Essay 예입니다. 무엇이 잘못됐는지 살펴봅니다.

Moving to Canada

When we moved to Canada last year, it was very hard on my family. We could not speak the language very well, we had no friends, and I was afraid to go to school.

When we arrived at the airport in Vancouver, we were very frustrated because we could not understand English very well. People spoke too quickly and they were hard to understand. They were rushing all over the place. Outside at the taxi stand we couldn't explain where we wanted to go and the driver misunderstood us and took us to the wrong hotel.

My family was all alone. My mother wanted to go back to Korea, but my father said that it would get better here. We went to a Korean restaurant and met many people who spoke our language. They invited us to come to their home the next day. When we arrived, there were many Koreans there and we were glad to have made some friends.

I went to school the first day and I was afraid. I couldn't find my classroom; I couldn't read my schedule; and I didn't have anyone to talk to.

Our first days in Canada were very difficult, but now we like living here very much.

This is not a good essay. Let's look at why!

1) Is there a **hook**?

> Answer: No

2) Write the sentence which contains the **thesis**.

> Answer: When we moved to Canada last year, it was very hard on my family

3) What are the three main ideas in the **blueprint**?

> Answer: 1) could not speak the language
> 2) had no friends
> 3) afraid to go to school

4) Which sentence in the first body paragraph contains information that is not relevant to the topic? Write the sentence here.

> Answer: They were rushing all over the place

5) List the supporting details that the writer uses in the first body paragraph to support his topic sentence.

> Answer: 1) talk too quickly for us to understand, 2) driver misunderstood us

6) What is wrong with the supporting details in the first body paragraph?

> Answer: There are only 2 supporting details and the writer needs to provide 3 details for each body paragraph.

7) In the second body paragraph, what is the topic sentence?

> Answer: My family was all alone.

Lesson 9: Structure of an Essay

8) What is wrong with the supporting details in the second body paragraph?

> Answer: The topic sentence talks about the family being alone, but the details talk about how they made lots of friends.

9) What is wrong with the supporting details in the third body paragraph?

> Answer: They are just listed and there is no explanation for them.

10) What is missing from the concluding paragraph of the essay?

> Answer: Although there is a reference back to the thesis, there is no mention of the blueprint.

11) What is good about the concluding paragraph?

> Answer: The writer makes a final comment about how he likes living in Canada now.

Look at the following revision of the essay:

Moving To Canada

Making a move at any time can be very hard for a family. However, moving to an entirely different country can create tremendous stress for everyone. When we moved to Canada last year, it was very hard on my family. We could not speak English very well and we had no friends there. For me, it was very frightening, especially when I had to go to school.

When we arrived at the airport in Vancouver, we were very frustrated because we could not understand English very well. We could not find our luggage, and even the kind woman who stopped to help us did not clearly understand what it was that we were looking for. When we talked to a security guard, he spoke too quickly and we didn't really understand what he said either. Finally, we found our luggage and made our way out of the airport. Outside at the taxi stand we couldn't explain where we wanted to go and the driver misunderstood us and took us to the wrong hotel. That day was one of the hardest days of our lives!

Not only was it difficult for us to communicate, but we also were all alone with no one to turn to for help. We had arranged to stay in a hotel for a few days and then move into our rented home. However, there was no one to take us to stores to shop for some furniture, nor was there anyone at the house to help us move things in. As well, when our other belongings arrived from Korea, we had no one to help us find the customs office. Finally when we were settled, we didn't know anyone to invite to our new home. My mother was so sad that she wanted to return to Korea.

Then the dreaded day arrived, and I had to go to school. On the first day I was so afraid that I thought I might be sick. When I entered the school, I couldn't find the office. When I finally did find it, the secretary gave me my schedule, but I couldn't read it. A student saw me looking very confused and told me where I would find my classroom, but again, I had trouble understanding him and I got lost several times before I finally arrived at the right place. Lunchtime was the very worst. I sat alone at a table in the cafeteria, and wondered if I would ever feel at home in this place.

Moving to a foreign country is very difficult. Language barriers and lack of friends make daily living hard. School is a special challenge for a foreign student. It certainly takes time and perseverance to adapt to a new culture.

Exercise 1

Here is an example of a five-paragraph essay. After you have finished reading the essay, complete the questions at the end.

As you read the following essay, think about what you have just learned about the structure of an essay.

1) Try to identify the **hook**, the **thesis** and the **blueprint**.
2) Did the body paragraphs each contain a topic sentence and three well-explained supporting details to prove the topic sentence?
3) Did the author remind you of the thesis and the main ideas in the conclusion?

The Disappointments of Television

I used to love watching television. I turned the TV on after dinner each night and settled in for an evening of great entertainment. Crime shows, game shows, reality shows, I knew them all! But lately, I have been constantly disappointed by the media I used to love. Watching television these days is a waste of time. There are too many commercial breaks, shows are unoriginal and programs are repeated far too often.

To begin with, I just don't like the constant interruptions for commercials. Two minutes after the opening credits, there is a series of ads. Then, ten minutes later, there is another group of commercials. To top it off, just before the end of the show, there is another break. And that's just for a thirty minute show! As if this were not bad enough, the commercial breaks are very long. It isn't a matter of watching one ad; there are usually a series of them. And often, the same ad appears twice or three times in the same break. I know that television shows need advertising to pay the cost of airing them, but lately ads have become more and more inane. Not only are there too many of them, they are all ridiculous! It appears as if the advertising community has run out of decent ideas and relies on stupidity to produce their commercials.

As well as endless advertising, I am finding that television shows lack any originality. Once a show is found to be popular, there are a dozen copycats that try to jump on the bandwagon and take advantage of the audience. One good example is the "reality show". When "Survivor" began, it was a new concept, and people were attracted by this different type of entertainment. However, now there are many imitators, and unfortunately, most of them are very poor. People live in an apartment together and the audience watches them interact with each other; a group of committed individuals are placed on an island and tempted to cheat on their partners; the bizarre family of a musician is put under the scrutiny of the public. This is just not good quality entertainment. Such imitation is everywhere on television. A crime series spawns a whole host of similar shows, with the only change being the city in which the crimes take place. And then there are the "Idol" shows. Contestants vie to be chosen the next music idol for their country, or the next supermodel, or the next dance champion or the next Donald Trump. The shows are all basically the same.

It isn't just the commercials, or the sameness of the shows that drive me crazy; it is also the fact that there are too many repetitions of programs. I get really annoyed when I settle in to see the next episode of my favorite situation comedy, only to find that it is the same show as last week's. And then, summer comes, and all the shows are repeats; nothing is new! You might as well turn off the television for the months of May to September. Then there are those channels that play the same program over and over again in the same day. Do the programmers think that the show is worth watching that many times?

It really is disappointing to turn on the television these days. Getting through a ton of commercials only to watch a boring reality show or a rerun just isn't worth the effort. I am going to find a library and take out a few good books to read in my future leisure time.

"The Disappointments of Television" is a good example of a standard short essay. It is a composition of over 500 words that consists of a one-paragraph introduction, a three-paragraph body, and a one-paragraph conclusion.

Questions

Introductory Paragraph

1) Which sentences provide the **hook** for the essay? Underline the sentences.

2) Write the sentence which states the **thesis** of the essay.

3) There is a **blueprint** in the introductory paragraph. List the three points that the writer will use to prove his/her ideas.

    a.

    b.

    c.

Body Paragraphs

4) Underline the topic sentence of the first body paragraph.

5) What are the three details given to support the topic sentence of the first body paragraph?

    a.

    b.

    c.

6) Underline the topic sentence of the second body paragraph.

7) What three details are given to support the topic sentence of the second paragraph?

   a.

   b.

   c.

8) Underline the topic sentence for the third body paragraph.

9) What three details are given to support the topic sentence of the third body paragraph?

   a.

   b.

   c.

Concluding Paragraph

10) Write down the sentence in the concluding paragraph which refers back to the thesis of the essay.

11) Underline the sentence which refers back to the blueprint in the introductory paragraph.

Look at the last sentence in the concluding paragraph. In this sentence, the writer has given a final thought about the topic. The writer has also persuaded the reader that there may be other activities (such as reading a good book) that could better fill the time than wasting leisure watching television.

✏️ Writing Exercise

Choose one of the following topics and write a five-paragraph essay. The essay must be 400-600 words in length. You may use the topic as your thesis statement for your essay.

You will find an essay outline sheet attached. You must fill out the outline before you begin to write.

Topics:

1. Computers are necessary for the modern student.

2. Sports are an important part of a child's education.

3. The driving age should be raised to twenty.

4. Movie going is now a thing of the past.

ESSAY OUTLINE

Thesis:

Three Main Ideas

*First_____

<u>Examples/Illustrations/Supporting Details</u>

1)
2)
3)

*Second_____

<u>Examples/Illustrations/Supporting Details</u>

1)
2)
3)

*Third_____

<u>Examples/Illustrations/Supporting Details</u>

1)
2)
3)

Lesson 10: Developing a Thesis

1. What is a Thesis?

> Thesis statement는 전체 essay의 topic sentence입니다. 즉, essay의 topic과 그에 대한 writer의 의견, 태도를 포함합니다. 아래는 효과적인 thesis statement를 쓰기위해 지켜야 할 5가지 rule입니다.

The thesis statement is the topic sentence for the entire essay. It states the **topic** that will be discussed in the essay, and also the writer's **attitude**, **opinion**, or **idea** about the topic. The thesis statement is broader than the topic sentence of a single paragraph and expresses the controlling idea for the entire essay. In fact, each of the body paragraphs will have a topic sentence that relates to the controlling idea in the thesis statement.

Here are five rules for the thesis statement which will help you write effectively.

1) **A thesis statement must not be written as a question**. Since the thesis statement is the directing statement for the entire essay, it should express a complete thought and therefore, must not be written as a question.

   Not a thesis statement: Do you have a fear of flying? (question)

   Thesis statement: My fear of flying has made travel difficult.

2) **A thesis statement expresses an opinion, attitude, or idea**, or idea; it does not simply announce the topic the essay will develop. When you are writing a thesis statement, you should avoid personal pronouns, such as "I".

   Not a thesis statement: I am going to discuss the consequences of stealing. (announcement of a topic)
   Thesis statement: The consequences of stealing can ruin one's life.

   Not a thesis statement: This essay will discuss the most popular kinds of books for children. (announcement of a topic)

<u>Thesis statement:</u>	The kinds of books that children really enjoy include fantasy, mystery and science fiction novels.
<u>Not a thesis statement:</u>	My thesis in this paper is how to handle teenagers. (announcement of a topic)
<u>Thesis statement:</u>	Handling a teenager is not often easy.

3) **A thesis statement should not express a fact.** Since the thesis statement expresses an attitude, opinion, or idea about a topic, the thesis statement is really a statement that someone could disagree with. The thesis statement, therefore, is a statement that needs to be explained or proved.

Not a thesis statement:	Chickens lay eggs. (express a fact.)
Thesis statement:	Chicken eggs are not good for one's health. (Someone could argue against this.)
Not a thesis statement:	There are both advantages and disadvantages to eating chicken eggs. (You are talking about both sides of the issue, so there is NO argument here.)
Not a thesis statement:	A lot of insects, weeds, and animals destroyed my garden last year. (express a fact)
Thesis statement:	Planting a garden can be a challenging experience.
Not a thesis statement:	There are many young people who are not good drivers. (express a fact)
Thesis statement:	There are many reasons why the driving age should be raised to 20.

4) **A thesis statement should express only one idea about a topic**; if a thesis statement contains two or more ideas, the writer is trying to prove more than one point, and the essay will likely lack coherence and unity.

Not a thesis statement:	Having friends over for a party is a great way to have fun and I have found some good recipes for party food.

Thesis statement: Hosting a party is fun.

5) **A thesis statement should be "just right" for the length of the essay.** Sometimes writers will choose thesis statements that are too broad, and cannot be developed in the short space of the essay. Some writers may choose a "dead end" thesis statement, one that is so narrow or limited that there is nothing much to say about it!

Not a thesis statement: In many ways, politics are important in our society. (too broad)

Thesis statement: Gambling has become a serious threat to many of Canada's poor people.

Not a thesis statement: Video games have a bad effect on people in a lot of ways. (too broad)

Thesis statement: Video games teach children to be violent, competitive and destructive.

Not a thesis statement: Working with the blind has taught me to appreciate my sight. (dead end, too narrow)

Thesis statement: My life has changed since I worked last summer with people who have no sight.

Exercise 1

Read the following sentences and decide whether or not they would make good thesis statements. Put a check mark beside the number of each one that would be a good thesis statement.

1) The difference between France and Belgium.
2) Senior citizens should not be allowed to drive.
3) There are many similarities and differences between Canada and Korea.
4) There are many advantages of a university education.
5) When I graduated from university, I couldn't find a job and I had a problem with my rent.

6) I am going to discuss my ideas about baseball.
7) Video games are not suitable for children.
8) Knowing how to cook is a valuable skill.
9) Why do I want to live in Canada?
10) I am going to talk about my job.
11) My summer vacation was a terrible waste of time.
12) I have to write three essays for my history class this semester.
13) Living in Canada is better than living in the United States.
14) My family is very difficult to live with.
15) I often like to go for a drive in the country.
16) Science Fiction is often about alien life in the universe.
17) How to catch a fish.
18) University is an interesting place to go.
19) Writing an essay is easier than you think.
20) Drinking tea is healthier than drinking coffee.

Exercise 2

Make each of the following statements into strong **thesis statements**. Remember the rules! If you have forgotten, look back at the explanations for help.

1) Police should have the power to be harder on people who speed and they should also demand bigger fines for speeders.

2) There are many similarities and differences between being a plumber and being an electrician.

3) The dangers of skiing.

4) Vancouver is one of Canada's largest cities.

5) I am going to discuss my views on buying a house.

2. Limiting a Topic

> 통상 topic은 일반적이며 광범위합니다. 이를 essay의 길이에 맞게 범위를 좁혀 구체적인 주제를 만드는 작업을 "Limiting a Topic"이라고 합니다.

Limiting a topic to make it work well for the length of essay that you want to write can take some work.

Imagine that your teacher has asked you to write an essay about "Family". Obviously, in a 500-word five-paragraph essay, you cannot cover all that can be said about your family! Do you talk about one person in your family? Do you talk about family vacations? Do you talk about your brothers, sisters, aunts, uncles?

You must make a decision.

The **General Subject** is: "**Family**". Let's limit it a bit. Suppose you decide that you are just going to talk about your brother. Then your **Limited Subject** is: "**My brother**".

Now, ask yourself: "What point do I want to make about my Limited Subject?" Perhaps you answer the question by saying: "My brother is the most interesting person in my family."

Now you have created a topic that you can prove! Can you think of three reasons why your brother is so interesting, and find at least three details to prove each point? If you can do that, then you have a good thesis statement and you are on your way to a strong essay.

 **Exercise 3**

For each of the General Subjects, write a Limited Subject.

General Subject	Limited Subject
1) Cell Phone	a. *Galaxy Note*
2) Travel	b.

3) Music c.

4) School d.

5) Television e

Now that you have your Limited Subjects, you are going to create a thesis statement to go with each one. Write your limited subjects below and then write a thesis statement for each one.

One way to create a thesis statement is to ask yourself a question about the Limited Subject.

For example: If my Limited Subject is "my mother", then I need to ask this question: "What point do I want to make about my mother?" My answer might be: "My mother is an amazing individual." Now I have created a thesis statement that can be proved.

Limited Subject	Thesis Statement
1) *Galaxy Note*	*Galaxy Note is an amazing device.*
2)	
3)	
4)	
5)	

3. Writing a Thesis Statement

> Thesis statement와 각 body paragraph의 topic sentence는 논리적인 연관을 가지고 있습니다. 앞서 배운 바와 같이 introductory paragraph (서론)의 blueprint는 thesis에 대한 3개의 main idea를 포함하며, 그 idea들은 각 body paragraph의 topic sentence로 쓰여집니다.

We can't say enough about the importance of thesis statements! So you will continue to be asked to write practice statements, and this time you will be given a chance to see and understand the logical relationship between a thesis statement and the topic sentences for each of the body paragraphs in the essay.

Remember that your blueprint in the introductory paragraph must reflect the three main ideas that are to be developed in the five-paragraph essay. Each body paragraph's topic sentence will restate one of these ideas, and then the supporting details in each paragraph will be used to prove the topic sentence.

The following activity will give you practice in writing an effective thesis statement. It will also give you practice in understanding the logical relationship between a thesis and the topic sentences of the body paragraphs in the essay.

 ### Exercise 4

Imagine that each of the statements below is a topic sentence for one of the body paragraphs in the essay. Decide what they have in common, what subject they are all talking about. Then, write a sentence that would be a good thesis statement for an essay containing the ideas in the topic sentences.

Here is an example:
   a. *Although the mall parking lots are huge, finding a place to park is almost impossible.*
   b. *Once you are in a store, finding a sales person to help you is always a chore.*
   c. *As well as insufficient sales people, the stores are always overcrowded.*

What is the common topic in all of these topic sentences? If you said, "Shopping at the mall," you're right! What is the writer's attitude to shopping at the mall? If you said, "He doesn't like it," then you're right again.

So, our thesis statement must include two elements:
   1. Mall shopping (topic)
   2. Does not like it (attitude)

Our thesis statement might be: "Shopping at the mall is never a pleasant experience." Here we see the topic and the attitude; each of the topic sentences will support this thesis.

Write a good thesis statement for each of the following groupings of topic sentences.

1) Thesis:_____

   a. My first vehicle was a motorcycle which reflected my rebellious teenage years.
   b. When I reached my twenties, I decided that a van would be the practical choice for my mature self.
   c. Now I have a small car, a sign that I am older and concerned about the cost of owning a vehicle.

2) Thesis:_____

   a. Going to university is a wise choice for someone who is looking for a professional career.
   b. Choosing a community college is a good idea for a person who would like to learn technical skills.
   c. Apprenticeship is the best decision for someone who would like to learn a trade.

3) Thesis:_____

   a. I first tried to lose weight by limiting the amount of food that I ate at each meal.
   b. For my second attempt at dieting, I decided to try a few of the weight loss products on the market.
   c. In my third attempt, I tried to stop eating, but that was the worst choice of all.

4) Thesis:_____

   a. The food is one of the best parts of this holiday.
   b. The holiday is a time for family visits.
   c. The holiday has music, lights and presents.

4. Supporting the Thesis with Specific Ideas

> Thesis statement를 support할 3개의 main idea들을 만드는 것을 공부합니다. 이 3개의 main idea는 introductory paragraph의 blueprint가 되며 또한 body paragraph들의 topic sentence가 됩니다.

After you have established your thesis statement, you need to develop ideas to support it. Sometimes ideas are easy to generate; other times, you must work hard to find good details.

Once you have brainstormed, you can use your ideas to create a trial outline. Write down a brief version of your thesis idea, and then decide which three main ideas you are going to use to support that thesis. It is important to choose ideas that are different from each other, and that can be supported by at least three specific supporting details.

Here is a "trial outline" for the essay you read about television watching.

> Brief Thesis Statement: Television is boring to watch.
> Ideas for Paragraphs:
> 1. There are too many commercials.
> 2. There are too many copycat shows.
> 3. There is nothing new.

 Exercise 5

Look at the following incomplete trial outlines. Add another point that could be used to develop the thesis statement. Make sure the point works logically with the others and that it is stated in **parallel structure** with the two points that are already listed.

> 1) The first day in a new job can be challenging.
>   a. meeting other employees
>   b. learning about the requirements of the job
>   c. _____
>
> 2) A good teacher has many positive qualities
>   a. understanding
>   b. patience
>   d. _____

3) The public pool is not the nicest place to spend the day.
    a. The facilities are often very dirty.
    b. The pool is often very crowded.
    e. _____

Questioning Method

> Idea를 만들어 내는 또 다른 방법은 thesis를 질문으로 바꾸어 보는 것입니다.

Another method of finding the ideas to prove your thesis statement is to turn your thesis into a question. Sometimes it may be difficult to get a start on your topics, so if you are having trouble generating ideas, try this method.

    a. Write down your thesis statement.
    b. Create a question from that statement using as many of the original words as possible. Using the words from the thesis makes you focus on the topic and the attitude you have expressed.

Look at this example:
    Thesis statement: "Watching television is boring."
    Question: "Why is watching television boring?"
    Now, let's answer the question:
    It is boring because: *there are too many commercials.*
                                      there are too many copycat shows.
                                      there is nothing new.

If you look back now at the trial outline above, you will see that we have come up with the same ideas.

Asking a question based on your thesis statement is a fast method of producing ideas. But you need to be sure that you focus not only on the topic, but also on the attitude toward the topic. In this case, the attitude is that television is "boring". So the answers will point out <u>why</u> television is boring.

If you don't have any answers to the question, then you need to reconsider your thesis!

Here is another example:

Thesis Statement: Growing up on a farm is the best environment for a child.
Question: Why is growing up on a farm the best environment for a child?
Our answers to this question need to focus on two things:
- *growing up on a farm*
- *the best environment*

Answers: *fresh country air*
home-grown food
learn to work with animals
get away from city pollution

The focus here is the attitude that there are benefits to living in a farm environment. So your answers need to reflect that attitude.

There are lots of answers to the question of why growing up on a farm is a better environment for a child. This indicates that you would have a lot of information to prove your thesis.

Exercise 6

For each of the following thesis statements:

a. State the thesis as a question which reflects the two answers that have been given.
b. Supply a third topic sentence which would appropriately answer the question that has been asked.

1) Thesis Statement: *The first day of school is hard for a child.*
   Question: _____
   Topic Sentences
   1. Leaving Mother at the door is difficult.
   2. Meeting the teacher is frightening.
   3.

2) Thesis Statement: *Exercise is important for good health.*
   Question: _____
   Topic Sentences
   1. Exercise gets your heart pumping.

  2. Exercise helps to control weight.
  3.

3) Thesis Statement: *Being an only child has its advantages.*
  Question: _____
  Topic Sentences
    1. You don't have to share with siblings.
    2. You get all the attention from your parents.
    3

Exercise 7

In this exercise, you will do the following:
  a. State the thesis as a question.
  b. Write three topic sentences which appropriately answer the question. Be sure to focus on both the topic and the writer's attitude to the topic.

1) Thesis Statement: *Learning a foreign language is very difficult.*
  Question: _____
  Topic Sentences
    1.
    2.
    3.

Thesis Statement: *Korea has some of the most beautiful places in the world.*
  Question: _____
  Topic Sentences
    1.
    2.
    3.

Thesis Statement: *The ability to play a musical instrument is a valuable skill.*
  Question: _____
  Topic Sentences
    1.
    2.
    3.

Exercise 8

Read the following essay and focus on identifying the various parts of the essay: hook, thesis statement, blueprint, and topic sentences of the body paragraphs.

Then answer the questions which follow the essay.

Grandparents

All parents enjoy the process of raising their children. Although there are both good times and difficult moments, watching children grow and develop is exciting and rewarding. While there is much to be said for parenthood, there is another stage of raising children that is even better. Being a grandparent is one of the greatest joys in a person's life. Grandparents can take their grandchildren to special places, tell them wonderful stories, and best of all, spoil them completely.

Taking grandchildren out for a day is a treat for both the children and the grandparents. Trips to the zoo, with explanations about animals, can be a learning experience as well as a time to enjoy together. Going to the park is fun too. Grandparents can push their grandchildren on the swings and play catch. Often a trip to a park means a picnic lunch with peanut butter and jelly sandwiches and lots of lemonade. There are so many wonderful places to visit!

Grandparents are very patient people and they have lots of time to read to their grandchildren. When they were parents, they were very busy, and often they could only read one story before bedtime. But as grandparents, they can read lots of stories and enjoy each one with their grandchildren cuddled close on their knees. But even better, grandparents can tell their grandchildren wonderful stories about the past and what it was like when they were just little children. Being a grandparent with time for a child is truly a joy.

The best part of being a grandparent is that you can spoil your grandchildren. Sometimes grandparents don't get to see their grandchildren very often, so when they visit, grandparents always have presents and treats for them. At Christmas and on birthdays, there are always lots of gifts from grandparents under the tree. When grandchildren visit, grandparents always have their favorite foods, and even when parents say no, sometimes grandparents will say yes! Spoiling children everyday is bad, but once in a while, it is fine, especially if it is grandparents who do the spoiling.

Being a grandparent is a special role in life. Spending time with grandchildren, talking to them and spoiling them is just part of the job. Being a parent is wonderful, but being a grandparent is a special treasure.

1) Underline the sentence(s) that provide the hook for this essay.

2) Write the thesis statement.

3) Write the blueprint for the essay.

4) What is the topic sentence for the first body paragraph? Underline the sentence.

5) What is the topic sentence for the second body paragraph? Underline the sentence.

6) What is the topic sentence for the third body paragraph? Underline the sentence.

✎ Writing Exercise

Choose one of the following topics and write a five-paragraph essay. You may use the statement as your thesis statement for your essay. You should be aiming for a length of 400-600 words.

You will find an essay outline sheet attached. You must fill out the outline before you begin to write.

1) The most important lessons in life cannot be learned in school.

2) Friendship is necessary for a happy life.

3) Being the oldest/youngest/middle child in a family brings a lot of special demands.

4) Using a cell phone can often be dangerous.

5) Our tomorrow will be better than today. Do you agree or disagree?

ESSAY OUTLINE

Thesis:

Thesis stated as a question:

Three Main Ideas
*First_____

      <u>Examples/Illustrations/Supporting Details</u>

1)
2)
3)

*Second_____

      <u>Examples/Illustrations/Supporting Details</u>

1)
2)
3)

*Third_____

      <u>Examples/Illustrations/Supporting Details</u>

1)
2)
3)

Lesson 11: Introduction and Conclusion

1. Writing an Introductory Paragraph

> 앞에서 배운 Introductory Paragraph의 구조에 대해 더 자세히 공부합니다. Introductory Paragraph는 Hook, Thesis Statement, Blueprint로 구성됩니다.

Here is an example of Introductory Paragraphs. Read carefully.

> *The ugly step-mother is a character in many children's fairy tales. But is this image of the step-mother fair? I am going to talk about step-mothers.*

Let's look at what is wrong with this introductory paragraph.

1) There is a short "**hook**". The writer has introduced the subject by talking about the fact that the "step-mother" is often a character in fairy tales and that maybe the image portrayed in these tales is unfair. But we need to extend the hook.

2) What is the **thesis statement** in this paragraph? There really isn't a strong thesis statement. Remember how we said earlier that the thesis statement had to be something that someone could argue with? Well, the statement "I am going to talk about step-mothers" does not provide any sense of debate. In fact, it is just an announcement of the topic, not a thesis statement at all.

3) There is absolutely no **blueprint**. When you are learning to write an essay, it is important to include the blueprint.

Let's rewrite the poor introductory paragraph.

Revised Introductory Paragraph:

> The step-mother is a character in many children's fairy tales. The image is always negative, as the woman is generally portrayed as ugly, unkind, and self-centered. But most stepmothers are not nasty, and fairy tales have given them an unjustifiable reputation. Stepmothers often have wonderful relationships with stepchildren, they do all the things that mothers do, and they can be friends as well as parents to their children.

We have added a longer **hook**. We have created a real **thesis statement** (most stepmothers are not nasty, and fairy tales have given stepmothers an unjustifiable reputation). And, we have added a **blueprint**.

2. Six Ways of Writing an Introductory Paragraph

> Introductory Paragraph의 Hook을 쓰는 데는 6가지 방법이 있습니다. 6가지 방법을 숙지하여 상황에 따라 적절한 방법을 쓸 수 있도록 합니다.

We have already talked about the importance of the introductory paragraph and the basic structure of the paragraph itself. There are several ways to write effective introductory paragraphs, and we are going to examine six of them.

2-1. General to Specific

> Topic의 일반적인 내용을 hook에서 서술한 후, 범위를 좁혀 thesis로 이어지고, 더 범위를 좁혀 blueprint의 main idea로 이어지는 방법.

This is the method that you have been using so far in these lessons. Basically, you begin with a general statement related to your general topic, then narrow it down to your thesis and then further narrow it down to your main ideas.

The general statement is your "hook". This statement introduces the subject in a broad way, and should involve at least two to three sentences. The next statement is your thesis in which you take the general subject and state what aspect of it you are going to discuss or prove in the essay. The final step is to narrow the thesis down by stating what three main ideas you will discuss in the essay.

Example:
(General Statement) Modern consumers have a huge range of children's toys from which to choose. (Narrowing towards the thesis) Many of these toys are excellent, but many are inadequate and even dangerous. (Thesis) Parents need to exercise great caution in selecting play items for their children. (Three ideas to be discussed–the "blueprint") They should choose toys that are safe, educational, and entertaining.

2-2. Question or a Series of Questions

> 질문으로 introductory paragraph를 시작하는 방법. 그 질문에 대한 답은 essay에서 하게 됩니다.

Another method is to begin with a question or two that will focus your reader on the topic of your essay. The idea is that you will answer these questions in your essay.

Example:

*(**Questions**) What is a mother? What makes a woman a good mother? (**Narrowing toward thesis**) The booming business of parenting guides and self-help books is one indicator of our society's preoccupation desire to find answers to these and related child-rearing questions. (**Thesis**) While individual mothers vary widely in personality, any good mother must be willing to focus her life on her children. (**Ideas to prove thesis– the "blueprint"**) A good mother provides healthy food for the body, guidance for the soul, and discipline for good living.*

2-3. Quotation

> 인용(quotation)으로 introductory paragraph를 시작하는 방법. 인용은 반드시 유명한 사람으로부터 하지 않아도 됩니다.

Often a quotation can be utilized to focus the reader's attention on the point you are going to make in your essay. The quotation does not have to come from a famous person; in fact, you might quote something a parent or friend has said, if the quotation is appropriate for your subject. You do need one or more sentences between the quotation and your thesis to create a smooth logical connection between them.

Example:

*(**Quotation**) "Since God could not be everywhere, he created mothers." (**Comment to show the relevance of the quotation**) This anonymous quotation pinpoints with gentle humor the importance of mothers in society. (**Thesis**) Mothers, in fact, are the most important members of families. (**Three ideas to prove the thesis– the "blueprint"**) Good mothers provide nourishment, guidance, and good fair discipline.*

2-4. Anecdote (anecdote: 일화, short and amusing story)

> 간략한 일화를 소개함으로써 introductory paragraph를 시작하는 방법. 일화는 2-3개 문장을 넘지 말아야 합니다.

In a few brief sentences, you can recount an anecdote (a very brief story) that will lead you into your thesis statement. The important thing, besides the relevance of the anecdote, is the brevity. Don't spend more than two or three sentences describing the story.

Example:

*(**Anecdote**) The mother took the hand of the crying child, bent down and gently spoke to her. Immediately, the child stopped crying. The mother smiled and the child hugged her. (**Comment to show the relevance of the anecdote**) We witness such incidents of motherly behavior every day and they warm the heart. (**Thesis**) Mothers are so important in society; in fact, they are the most important member of the family. (**Blueprint**) They provide nourishment, guidance, and sound discipline for growing children.*

2-5. Opposite

> 반대의견을 먼저 소개함으로써 introductory paragraph를 시작하는 방법.

You can start your essay by using a point opposite to the one you are going to make. This will surprise your readers and keep them reading. This technique also shows that you have considered the opposing arguments and still believe your position is the most compelling one.

Example:

*(**Opposite**) Some people believe that the most important member of the family is the father. (**Expansion upon initial statement**) After all, he often is the only wage earner; he is generally stronger physically than other members of the family; and he makes many of the significant decisions for the family. (**Thesis**) But despite his contributions, it is not the father, but the mother who is the heart and soul of the family. (**Blueprint**) She is the one who nourishes, guides and disciplines the children into becoming solid members of society.*

2-6. Amazing Statistic/Fact

> 독자의 흥미를 끄는 사실, 통계자료를 소개함으로써 introductory paragraph를 시작하는 방법.

You can begin your essay by stating a fact or statistic that will amaze or startle your reader. Your fact, if well chosen, will likely persuade your readers that it is important for them to go on and hear what you have to say.

Example:

(Introductory fact) Do you believe that having one drink after work does not impair your ability to drive? Well, think again! Seventy-five per cent of vehicle accidents in the United States involve a driver who has had at least one drink! Such accidents can be prevented. ***(Thesis)*** It is time to ban drivers with any alcohol intake from getting behind the wheel of their cars. ***(Blueprint)*** The law, the bar owners, and the drivers themselves must assist in the prevention of alcohol-related accidents.

 Exercise 1

Write an introductory paragraph for each of the following topics, using the method stated.

1) Topic: Advertising
   Method: Opposite

2) Topic: Movies
   Method: Quotation

3) Topic: Obesity (obesity: 비만)
   Method: Statistic / Fact

4) Topic: Advertising
   Method: General to Specific

5) Topic: Movies
   Method: Question

6) Topic: Obesity
   Method: Anecdote

3. Three Ways of Writing a Concluding Paragraph

> Concluding paragraph (결론)을 쓰는 방법은 3가지가 있습니다. 앞의 내용을 단순히 summary하거나 thesis와 main idea를 반복하는 것은 좋은 conclusion이 아닙니다. 좋은 conclusion은 thesis를 새로운 방법으로 restate하고 독자로 하여금 앞서 전개된 내용에 대해 다시 한번 생각하게 하는 것입니다.

The conclusion of your essay is as important as all the other parts. You have worked very hard to create an excellent essay, so it deserves an excellent completion.

Your conclusion is a chance to give your reader an opportunity to think about what you had to say. Like the introduction, it gives your reader focus and emphasis. If your conclusion is dull, repetitive or simply a summary of your essay, then you have not taken full advantage of the potential value of your conclusion.

Although there should be a sense of summary, simply repeating the thesis and your main ideas is ineffective.

A good conclusion will restate in a new way the thesis of the essay and ask the reader to think about and assess the ideas you have presented. If you do choose to refer to the main ideas again in the conclusion, then you should use this reference to encourage the reader to think beyond what has already been stated.

Your conclusion should convince your reader that your ideas are good and deserve further consideration.

3-1. Mirror Ending

> Thesis를 다른 방법으로 restate하여 독자로 하여금 essay 내용에 대해 다시 생각하게 하는 방법.

This kind of conclusion allows you to restate your thesis in a new way and refer back to the ideas that you have made. However, you need to go further and make your thesis and ideas relevant to your reader. Simply restating your introductory paragraph is a waste of your conclusion and also is a boring repetition of ideas. You should not introduce new ideas at this point, but there are ways of getting your reader to think about the ideas you have already stated.

> **Example:**
> *Mothers are the truly significant members of our families because they provide so many of the*

basic requirements for their children's growth and well-being. It is not surprising that we celebrate motherhood with gifts and cards to let the most important members of our family know that we love and appreciate them.

3-2. Questions

> 독자에게 질문을 던짐으로써 essay의 내용을 다시 한번 생각하게 하는 방법.

To make your reader think more about what you have said, you can ask several relevant questions that will get them considering your ideas.

Example:
What would society be without the influence of mothers? Who could provide the care and guidance that is such a vital part of a mother's job description? In a society fraught with more dangers than ever before, and more temptations for children, it is even essential to have the influence of a strong mother figure. A Mothers' role in the family and society has never been more important for the world.

3-3. Call for Action or Prediction about the Future

> 어떤 action을 취할 것을 언급하거나, 그 action이 없을 경우 발생할 결과를 예측함으로써 concluding paragraph를 쓰는 방법.

This kind of conclusion allows you to ask your reader to consider doing something about the topic of your essay. It also allows you to predict the dangers of not acting on your ideas.

Here are two examples:

1) Mothers are the most important people in the family, and yet, motherhood is less revered now than in the past. As women return to the workforce soon after the birth of their children, the dynamic of the family changes, and the true concepts of motherhood are often lost. But this shift will have a considerable impact on our social fabric. A working mother is a fact in many societies today, and no one is suggesting a return to the early years of the housewife/mother of years gone by. However, it is important to remember what mothers provide for their children and never lose track of the significance that they have within their families.

2) If people considered each purchase they made in terms of their budget, there would be fewer incidents of bankruptcy. Too often people act on their need for immediate gratification, and suspend their common sense. This practice leads to financial difficulties and often to extreme stress both for the individual and his or her family. Budgeting is not a difficult chore, and it can be an invaluable tool with which to organize your life and increase your happiness.

 Exercise 2

What type of conclusion is being used in each of the following? Write your answer in the space provided.

1) What can we expect from a world that allows terrorists to function? Surely we will only see more horrors, more bloodshed, more needless suffering.

2) Some people work all their lives to achieve fame and fortune. They want to be recognized and applauded by the world. But a famous person gives up so much to fulfill this dream. They often live in fear, are hounded by the media, and worry always that they will lose their status with the public. It is better to be an ordinary person than to lead a life so filled with stress.

3) When we lose someone we care about, the devastation is often overwhelming. We may feel depressed, sorrowful, or isolated. We must try to remember that life goes on, and that we need to regroup and forge ahead despite our loss.

✎ Writing Exercise

Choose one of the following topics. On the outline sheet provided, write a thesis and turn it into a question to find the supporting ideas. Write the topic sentences in the spaces provided.

Be sure to write a well-developed five-paragraph essay with enough specific detail to make your essay interesting and convincing. Your essay must be 400-600 words in length.

Reread the 6 methods of introduction and the 3 methods of conclusion. Decide which method you will use to introduce and which method you will use to conclude. Write your choices on the outline sheet.

Topic / Subject	Limited Subject	Thesis Statement
1. Games		
2. Diet		
3. Teachers		
4. Social Network		
5. Heroism		

ESSAY OUTLINE

Thesis:

Thesis stated as a question:

Method of Introduction:

Three Main Ideas
*First_____
<u>Examples/Illustrations/Supporting Details</u>
1)
2)
3)

*Second_____
<u>Examples/Illustrations/Supporting Details</u>
1)
2)
3)

*Third_____
<u>Examples/Illustrations/Supporting Details</u>
1)
2)
3)

Method of Conclusion:

Lesson 12: Connecting Ideas with Transitions

1. Transitions

> Transition은 idea와 idea를 논리적이고 부드럽게 연결하는 연결사입니다. 즉, 도로에서의 교통표시판과 같은 역할입니다. 적절한 transition의 사용은 essay에서 idea간의 smooth한 전환을 위한 중요한 사항입니다.

"Transition" means to move from one thing to another. When we refer to transitions in an essay, we are talking about those words, phrases, and even sentences that guide the reader from idea to idea in the essay. Transitions should not be underestimated. They are important tools for the writer to use in his/her effort to ensure that the reader is led smoothly through the thoughts of the essay.

As you drive along a road, you see signs that tell you what you should do, what you should look out for, or which way to proceed. Transitions in an essay are like road signs. They tell the reader when things are changing or moving in a certain direction.

The following is a list of the common transitions grouped according to the kind of "signal" they give to readers. Some transitions can be used for more than one kind of signal.

1) <u>Addition Signals</u>: one, first of all, second, the third reason, also, next, another, and, in addition, moreover, furthermore, finally, last of all

   These signals give you a sequential and often numerical order for ideas.

2) <u>Time Signals</u>: first, then, next, after, as, before, while, meanwhile, soon, now, during, finally, immediately, previously, simultaneously, later

   Time signals are like Addition Signals in that they point out an order. However the focus in this type of signal is the 'time frame'.

3) <u>Space Signals</u>: next to, across, on the opposite side, to the left, to the right, above, below, near, nearby

   These signals might be used if you were giving directions or if you were describing a location or a picture.

4) <u>Change-of-Direction Signals</u>: but, however, yet, in contrast, although, otherwise, still, on the contrary, on the other hand, nevertheless

These signals tell the reader that you are going to give another opinion, often one that is opposed to the one you have expressed. Look for a change in the way a subject is being approached.

5) <u>Illustration Signals</u>: for example, for instance, specifically, as an illustration, such as

These signals tell the reader that there is an example coming up.

6) <u>Conclusion Signals</u>: therefore, hence, consequently, so, thus, then, as a result, in summary, to conclude, last of all, finally, accordingly

These signals indicate a conclusion, a result, and a final point that is being made.

Read the following paragraph. The transitional expressions are in italics.

> Whenever I go back to my hometown, I have some mixed feelings. *First of all*, I like to visit the house I grew up in. The new owners have kept it much the same as I remember it in my childhood, *although* the trees in the yard are taller, and the front steps have been replaced. *Recently*, the new occupants have built a garage at the side of the house, and the sandbox and garden swing that used to be there have disappeared. *In addition* I notice that the old oak tree with the remnants of an old wood tree house has been removed and in its place is a small pond, filled with water lilies and gold fish. *Gradually*, I turn and walk away. This is someone else's home now, and they too must be filling it with their memories. *Perhaps* they too will come back one day to see the changes that have been made in their old home.

Each transitional expression in this paragraph precisely links the sentence it is in to the one before.

- The paragraph begins with the writer explaining what he did *first*.
- He says that the place looks familiar *although* it is not exactly the same.
- Then he points out something that has been done *recently* to change the house.
- In the third sentence, the writer *adds* a detail to what he has said before.
- Then he tells you what he did next.
- At the end, he uses the word *perhaps* to link his experience with the visit to what may happen in the future to the present owners of the house.

We often use transitions naturally in our speech and in our writing. But it is particularly important to be sure that transitions are present to help the reader visualize the thought process in the writing.

Exercise 1

1) Underline the four *addition* signals in the following selection:

    To build a campfire, you need to follow several steps. First of all, you need to find a location that is safe. Do not light fires under trees or in areas where the ground is covered by debris from trees and plants. This material can easily burst into flame and cause difficulties. Next, you need to find some dry kindling. These are small, thin pieces of wood that can burn easily and provide fuel for larger pieces of wood. Place these pieces in a bundle in the area that you have chosen for your fire. In addition, you might want to add some dry leaves to the kindling, but if there is a wind blowing, these pieces may fly off into areas that can catch fire. Light your fire with a match. Finally, when the fire begins to burn, you should add several larger pieces of wood.

2) Underline the five *time* signals in the following selection:

    When you go for a job interview, there are several things to remember if you want to be successful. First, you should dress appropriately. Choose an outfit that is clean, smart, and businesslike. Do not wear at hat! Next, bring an up-to-date resume with you. The resume should be printed on good quality paper, and should accurately reflect your educational and employment history. Before you enter the interview room, you should check your appearance in a mirror. Is your hair tidy? Is your face clean? While you are in the interview, speak up, speak clearly, and think carefully before you answer. Don't interrupt the interviewer. Finally, when you leave the interview, be sure to thank the person for seeing you.

3) Underline the five *space* signals in the following selection:

    I have worked very hard to organize my garden. Next to the house, I have planted large flowering shrubs that protect the rest of the garden from the wind. These shrubs have beautiful yellow flowers that blossom all summer and give the garden a blaze of color. To the left is my vegetable garden. It is filled with tomatoes, green peppers, onions, and carrots. The runner beans are on the right of the garden. There they grow along the rocks and over the wood pile! On the opposite side, I have planted an herb garden. Here there is basil, oregano, parsley, sage, and rosemary. When these herbs mature, I cut them and take them into the house where I dry them and bottle them for use during the winter. Near the herb garden is a small flower garden; however, I have not been very successful growing flowers. Each year, the local deer eat most of the blooms. Nevertheless, I plant the seeds each year, and even though I never get to enjoy the flowers, I do enjoy watching the deer as they sneak into my garden to eat!

4) Underline the four *change-of-direction* signals in the following selection:

Many people enjoy taking their children to the zoo. It is a chance for children to see animals that they would not be able to see anywhere else. However, I find the zoo a depressing place to visit. I know that the animals are well fed and safe from harm in a zoo setting. Still, I hate to see them cooped up in small cages, unable to run or fly freely as they would in the wild. The zoo is certainly a place where we can learn about the habits of wild animals and birds and such an education is valuable for both children and adults. Yet, it seems somehow cruel to put our educational needs above the needs of the animals that are captive for us. What if the situation were reversed? What if animals put us in cages for observation? The thought itself is claustrophobic! The zoo is a popular place, but it is not a place that I intend to visit again.

5) Underline the three *illustration* signals in the following selection:

Magazine covers are designed to encourage people to buy the book. For example, the cover of one popular magazine recently pictured a famous actress. The text on the cover indicated that there were more pictures inside, as well as a tell-all interview with the actress about her recent divorce. The magazine sold so quickly that one store had sold out their stock in the first two days! Tabloids such as you see at the checkout counters in supermarkets also design their covers to attract attention. For instance, they often have stories about alien babies, two-headed animals, and sightings of Michael Jackson. Despite the foolishness of these headlines, people amazingly buy the papers.

6) Underline the two *conclusion signals* in the following selection:

When I decided to quit school at the end of grade eleven, I thought that it would be easy to find a job and get on with my life. I was so wrong! My first interview was a disaster. I arrived at the company with my resume. I had had several part-time jobs while I was at school, and was confident that I would be able to find full-time work. Consequently, I found it shocking when the interviewer told me that the job I was applying for required a high school diploma. After all, it was just a job in the mail room, sorting and distributing mail to the employees of the company. Why would I need a diploma to do that? I looked for weeks, but all other job interviews were much the same as the first one. As a result, I knew I had no other choice but to go back to school.

2. Transitional Sentences

> Transition은 단어, 구 뿐만 아니라 문장으로 이루어 지기도 합니다. 이러한 Transitional Sentence는 essay에서 paragraph를 연결하는 역할을 하며 다음의 2가지가 있습니다.

Transitions can be made with whole sentences as well as single words or phrases. These *transitional or linking sentences are* used to tie paragraphs together in an essay. The *transitional sentence* can be used in two ways:

1) First Sentence in a Paragraph

Here are two paragraphs from the essay in Lesson 10 "The Disappointments of Television". Read it again carefully and note the underlined sentence in the second paragraph.

    To begin with, I just don't like the constant interruptions for commercials. Two minutes after the opening credits, there is a series of ads. Then, ten minutes later, there is another group of commercials. Then, just before the end of the show, there is another break. And that's just for a thirty-minute show! Add to that, the commercial breaks are very long. It isn't a matter of watching one ad; there are usually a string of them. And often, the same ad appears twice or three times in the same break. I know that television shows need advertising to pay the cost of airing them, but lately ads have become more and more inane. Not only are there too many of them, they are all ridiculous! It appears as if the advertising community has run out of decent ideas and relies on stupidity to produce their commercials.

    <u>As well as endless advertising, I am finding that television shows lack any originality.</u> Once a show is found to be popular, there are a dozen copycats that try to jump on the bandwagon and take advantage of the audience. One good example is the "reality show". When "Survivor" began, it was a new concept, and people found it a different type of entertainment. However, now there are many imitators, and unfortunately, most of them are very bad. People live in an apartment together and the audience watches them interact with each other; a group of committed individuals are placed on an island and tempted to cheat on their partners; the bizarre family of a musician is put under the scrutiny of the public. This is just not entertainment. This imitation is everywhere on television. A crime series spawns a whole host of similar shows, with the only change being the city in which the crimes take place. And then there are the "Idol" shows. Contestants vie to be chosen the next music Idol for their country, or the next supermodel, or the next dance champion or the next Donald Trump. The shows are all the same.

The underlined sentence refers back to the point being made in the first paragraph – *the endless advertising*. It also serves as a topic sentence for the next paragraph by introducing the next point – *shows lack any originality*. The writer has used this sentence as a transition, tying the two paragraphs together.

2) Last Sentence in a Paragraph

Read the same two paragraphs from "The Disappointments of Television".

This time, the essay has been slightly reworded to use the last sentence of the first paragraph as a transitional sentence rather than the first sentence of the second paragraph. As well, the first sentence of the second paragraph has also been slightly altered to accommodate the changes.

    To begin with, I just don't like the constant interruptions for commercials. Two minutes after the opening credits, there is a series of ads. Then, ten minutes later, there is another group of commercials. Then, just before the end of the show, there is another break. And that's just for a thirty-minute show. Add to that, the commercial breaks are very long. It isn't a matter of watching one ad; there are usually a string of them. And often, the same ad appears twice or three times in the same break. I know that television shows need advertising to pay the cost of airing them, but lately ads have become more and more inane. Not only are there too many of them, they are all ridiculous! It appears as if the advertising community has run out of decent ideas and relies on stupidity to produce their commercials. <u>However, the annoyance of the commercials is nothing compared with the unoriginality of the shows themselves!</u>

    <u>There simply are no innovative shows these days.</u> Once a show is found to be popular, there are a dozen copycats that try to jump on the bandwagon and take advantage of the audience. One good example is the "reality show". When "Survivor" began, it was a new concept, and people found it a different type of entertainment. However, now there are many imitators, and unfortunately, most of them are very bad. People live in an apartment together and the audience watches them interact with each other; a group of committed individuals are placed on an island and tempted to cheat on their partners; the bizarre family of a musician is put under the scrutiny of the public. This is just not entertainment. This imitation is everywhere on television. A crime series spawns a whole host of similar shows, with the only change being the city in which the crimes take place. And then there are the 'Idol' shows. Contestants vie to be chosen the next music Idol for their country, or the next supermodel, or the next dance champion or the next Donald Trump. The shows are all the same.

Exercise 2

Now try writing some transitional sentences. Below you will find thesis statements and brief sentence outlines of essays. The sentences for the second and third paragraphs will serve as transitional sentences in the way that you observed in the examples above.

In the blanks, you are required to add the words needed to complete the topic sentences so that they reflect the ideas in the previous paragraph and introduce the idea of the next paragraph.

In order to do this, you must look at the blueprint (the three main ideas listed in the thesis).

1)

Thesis	The most important things that I have learned from my mother are patience with others, self-discipline, and kindness.
First body Paragraph	First, my mother taught me that it is important to be patient with others.
Second body Paragraph	In addition to teaching me about the importance of _____, my mother taught me the value of _____.
Third body Paragraph	As well as the value of _____ my mother emphasized the benefits of _____.

2)

Thesis	Expensive gasoline, rising insurance costs, and high maintenance rates make it reasonable for young people to use public transportation rather than own cars.
First body Paragraph	For one thing, gasoline prices have increased significantly over the past few years.
Second body Paragraph	In addition to rising gas prices, _____ make car ownership difficult.
Third body Paragraph	Even more important than _____ and _____, though, is the cost of _____, which makes public transportation more reasonable than car ownership.

Lesson 12: Connecting Ideas with Transitions **173**

3)

Thesis	Cleaner air, quiet surroundings, and slower pace make living in the country healthier than living in the city.
First body Paragraph	First of all, living in the country lets you _____.
Second body Paragraph	Besides _____, living in the country is _____.
Third body Paragraph	Finally, the _____ of country living makes it a healthier place to be.

Exercise 3

Read the following body paragraphs. Assume that the three paragraphs occur after an introductory paragraph in an essay. Change the first sentence of the second and third paragraphs so that they become **transitional sentences** between the paragraphs.

One of the things that I do to relax is listening to music. Softer country music will often take the day's stress away. I find myself tapping my toes or humming a song and the day's tension is forgotten in the music. Another kind of music that releases my tension is soft rock. Again I find myself lost in a recognized tune that makes me let go of all the day's events. But I find that the best music to release tension is classical. The sounds of Beethoven's symphonies, Handel's Water Music or Brahms' lullabies are soothing. As I listen I can feel my body relax and the tension in my muscles dissolve. My neck moves without pain again, and my shoulders feel soft and liberated.

I like to do yoga to relax. The gentle exercise allows me to focus my body on areas that are tightened by stress. I can feel the tension release, especially in my neck and arms. My body bends and stretches until I move freely and without pain. Another type of relaxation that I enjoy is tai chi. I love to stand in the garden by my pond and move to the gentle rhythm of the wind. Tai chi lets me feel the natural world around me as my body releases the cares and stresses of the world. Most of all, I love to meditate to help relieve stress. Alone in the quiet of my room, I ponder all the good things in the world and imagine a shaded place beside a small brook, where I can sit and hear only the sounds of water, the wind and the birds.

1) The first sentence is changed to: _____

_____

I often exercise to get rid of stress. If I choose to go to the gym, I like to run on the treadmill with my portable disc player plugged into my ears. I run to the beat of the music, while blocking out the sounds of clanging weights and people talking and shouting to each other. Or, I go down to my basement where I have a stationary bicycle and once again with my earphones clamped into my ears, I ride the bike and dream of beautiful places and warm sunny days. Most of all, I like to walk in the country to breathe the fresh air and see the joys of the natural world. How can anyone feel stress in such a beautiful place?

2) The first sentence is changed to:_____

_____

 Exercise 4

In the spaces provided, add appropriate transitions to tie together the sentences and ideas in the following essay. Use the words in the box to fill the blanks, but use each only once.

Annoying People

Attending a sports event should be a pleasant experience for the spectator. After all, he has usually paid a high price for his ticket, and therefore should be allowed to sit and enjoy his day. However, sports games seem to attract a number of people that help to make the day unpleasant. The talker can be annoying, but worse is the screamer and worst of all, the drinker.

1)

| Then | First of all | Another | However |

_____, there is the talker. This is the person who sits behind you and needs to comment on each play that has been made. He seems to believe that everyone around him is interested in his version of the game. _____ there are those who need to keep in touch with everyone they know by cellphone. They talk endlessly throughout the game, reliving for the person on the other end of the line each play that occurs in the game. _____type of talker is the one who really has no interest at all in the game. He or she spends the entire game discussing the latest gossip. Fans are treated to personal stories as well as all the latest "dirt" on famous celebrities. _____ the very worst type of talker is the one who whines. He or she is annoyed about the location of the seats, the height of the fans in front of them, the taste of the beer, the size of the popcorn box, and even the color of the team's uniform! Nothing pleases this person, and they are happy to let the world around them know about it!

2)

| On the contrary   Then   As a result   After   Second |

  The _____ category of fan is the type who screams. They scream each time their own team scores a goal or touchdown. They scream whenever a member of their team makes a good play. They just like to scream. _____ there are the ones who scream for both teams. They jump in the air at any play whatsoever, vocalizing their delight (or is it anger?). Every game play requires a scream. _____ they often lose their voices part way through the game, and one would think that silence would reign. _____ after the intermission, they seem to rally and scream once again for the remainder of the game. _____ sitting in front of a screamer for one game, a person would think twice about attending another game.

3)

| In addition to   But   Last of all |

  _____ there is the drinker. He is the worst of the worst! _____ talking, and screaming, he is also drinking far too much, and so his words are often slurred, louder, and more brazen than either of the first two categories of people. _____ that is not the worst problem with the drinker. The more he drinks, the more clumsy he becomes. He will often spill his drinks on other patrons, and in his worst condition will fall over because his co-ordination fails him. He makes a complete fool of himself, but at the same time he makes those around him feel uncomfortable and often angry.

✏️ Writing Exercise

Choose one of the following topics. On the outline sheet provided, write a thesis and turn it into a question to find the supporting ideas. Write the topic sentences in the spaces provided.

Be sure to write a well-developed five-paragraph essay with enough specific detail to make your essay interesting and convincing. Your essay must be 400-600 words in length.

Use **TRANSITIONS** to connect your paragraphs and within the paragraphs themselves to make your meaning clear.

Reread the 6 methods of introduction and the 3 methods of conclusion. Decide which method you will use to make an interesting beginning and a convincing ending. Write your decisions on the outline sheet.

Topics:

1. Life's best goals.
2. The lessons of failure.
3. My favorite holiday.
4. My most embarassing moment
5. The best day of my life

ESSAY OUTLINE

Thesis:

Thesis stated as a question:

Method of Introduction:

Three Main Ideas
*First_____

    Examples/Illustrations/Supporting Details

-
-
-

*Second_____

    Examples/Illustrations/Supporting Details

-
-
-

*Third_____

    Examples/Illustrations/Supporting Details

-
-
-

Method of Conclusion:

> 이번 lesson부터는 essay의 5가지 type에 대해 공부하면서 앞에서 배운 lesson들을 적용하고 응용하도록 합니다. Essay의 type이란 essay를 전개해 나가는 방식을 의미합니다.
> – Persuasive /Argumentative Essay
> – Cause and Effect Essay
> – Definition Essay
> – Division and Classification Essay
> – Comparison and Contrast Essay

Lesson 13: Persuasive/Argumentative Essay – Part 1

> 이번 lesson에서는 설득 또는 자기의 주장, 의견을 펴는 Persuasive /Argumentative Essay를 공부합니다. Persuasive/Argumentative Essay는 TOEFL 등의 writing test에서 흔히 요구되는 essay type입니다. 이 type의 essay에서는 서로 상반되는 의견이 있는 topic이 주어지고 그에 대해 자신의 의견이나 주장을 펴게됩니다.

The **persuasion** essay is probably one of the most common types of writing that will be required of students at high school, college and university. Sometimes, persuasive essays are called **argumentative** essays.

1. What is Persuasion?

When you argue with a friend or with a family member, or when you try to convince someone to believe that your opinion is the best one, you are engaging in **persuasion**. To persuade is to convince someone that a particular opinion or point of view is the correct one.

One of the major mistakes that people make when they argue is to depend on emotional, misleading, or even false arguments. If you want to borrow your parents' car on a Saturday night, you might have to persuade your parents that they should allow you to use it. Giving them some sensible arguments – you will be home on time, you won't drink and drive, you won't fill the car with too many people, you will call them if you need to, you will not let someone else drive the car – will help your parents to see that you are sensible and honest. However, if you simply stamp your feet and whine that everyone else can have their parents' car to drive, and that it isn't fair that you can't have the car, then you have slipped into an emotional argument that is simply not convincing!

2. Methods of Persuasion

> Persuasion을 하는 5가지 방법에 대해 공부합니다.

There are several ways to persuade in writing. Although you will not use all of these in the same paragraph, you must know how to use each one, if the situation demands it. When you begin to write essays, you will be able to use several methods of persuasion in the same essay.

In this lesson, we will look at **five methods** used in writing a persuasion paragraph.

2-1. Using Facts

> 믿을 만한 출처(source)의 사실(fact)을 인용하여 설득합니다.

A fact simply states something that **is**. Facts should appeal to people's intelligence, and they should come from dependable sources. Facts should not play on the emotions. Facts are simply statements of what is.

For example, if you want to prove that smoking damages health, then you might look for supporting facts from pamphlets found at a doctor's office or in the hospital. Since most of us do not read medical books or magazines where the language is geared for medical personnel, and we are likely not writing for a medical audience, we should try to find sources that speak to the general public. Facts must be **clear**, and the source of information must be **reliable**.

Look at this 'fact' from a persuasion paragraph:
 Everyone knows that the Ford Motor Company is the leader in sales of trucks in Canada.

In the example above, there is no source listed. The writer's 'fact' is not supported at all. Who is making this statement? Why should the reader believe it?

Look at the difference here:
 According to the July 2011 report in The Consumer's Guide to Automobiles, the Ford Motor Company is the leader in sales of trucks in Canada.

In this sentence, the writer has given the reader the name of the magazine, and the date of the report on which the fact was based. It will be up to the reader to decide if the source is dependable, but at least the reader knows that the information is documented, not invented by the writer.

2-2. Refer to an Authority

> 해당분야의 권위있는 사람 또는 기관의 information을 인용하여 설득합니다.

A person who is an authority on something is an expert. An expert can be relied on to give unbiased facts and information based on his or her knowledge of a subject.

If you want to convince someone that smoking is bad for health, you would rely on the information provided by a doctor, or by the Lung Association. These are experts in the field.

If you want to convince someone that head injuries in contact sports are rising, then you would give information provided by coaches, hospitals and doctors. These are people who would actually know enough about the subject to give credible facts.

Don't appeal to sources just because they are famous or interesting. Wayne Gretzky (famous Canadian hockey player) may know a lot about sports, but he may not know a lot about cars. So if you were trying to convince your reader that a certain brand of car was the best to buy, you would not use Wayne Gretzky as an expert in the field. You are aware that advertisers use celebrities to try and sell their products, but unless the celebrity has some expertise in the field he or she is advertising, then the advertising is not based on solid fact. Your writing must be based on credible facts.

2-3. Using Examples

> 근거있고 관련된 사례(examples)들을 들어 설득합니다.

You have been using examples in paragraphs that you have written so far and it is also important to use them when you write persuasion/argument paragraphs. What you must remember, as we have stressed in the past, is that the example must clearly relate to the topic sentence and it should be typical of the situation.

For example, if you want to convince your reader that high schools should ban contact sports because the number of head injuries is rising each year, then you might say:

> *"Johnson High School, for instance, recorded four serious head injuries in 2009. In 2010, eight boys received serious concussions (뇌진탕), and in 2011, there were ten boys with serious head injuries, two of them serious enough to require long term hospitalization. Other high schools are reporting similar results over the same time period."*

Avoid using examples that are not really typical of the situation. Just because one boy hit his head in football practice does not mean that contact sports should be banned altogether.

2-4. Predicting the Consequence

> 예견되는 결과를 언급하면서 설득합니다.

When a writer predicts the consequence, he is helping the reader to see what would happen if something does, or does not, occur.

For example, you might want to convince your reader that we must stop polluting our atmosphere. To do this, you could predict the consequence by saying that "if we continue to pollute the atmosphere with toxic gases, we will eventually destroy the protective ozone layer which surrounds the earth."

Avoid exaggerating the consequence:
For instance, telling the reader "if we continue to pollute the atmosphere with toxic gases, we will destroy all life on earth" exaggerates the consequences. The reader is going to be understandably suspicious of your conclusions and the rest of what you have to say may not be taken seriously.

2-5. Answering the Opposition

> 반대의견을 인지하고 틀린 점을 지적하여 설득합니다.

Not everyone is going to agree with what you have to say. In fact, that is the whole point of a persuasive/argumentative paragraph. In this type of writing, you take a stand on a controversial issue, and prove your side of the argument. So as your readers goes through your paragraph, they may be forming arguments in their own mind to counter or disagree with your point of view. One tactic used by writers is to acknowledge that there are arguments against what you are saying. Once you have acknowledged the opposition, then you need to go on and prove that the opposition is wrong.

For example, if you wanted to prove that the candidate that you are supporting is the best choice for leader, but you know that people oppose the choice because the candidate did not go on to post secondary education, then you might make the following statement to acknowledge that there is opposition to your point of view. Then you need to counter the opposition by showing why it is wrong.

"Although some will argue that my candidate does not have a lot of education, they should consider that many of the world's greatest leaders, including Winston Churchill, were not necessarily brilliant scholars"

The statement **acknowledges** the candidate's lack of education, but it also **counters** that opposition by saying that some of the best world leaders have not been well educated. It even names one of the most outstanding world leaders who struggled with education.

One of the dangers of acknowledging the opposition is the temptation to attack those who do not believe as you do. It is fine to attack their ideas, but it is absolutely wrong to attack their character!

Avoid statements like the following:
  "Any fool knows that…"
  "To believe in that, you have to be a crook yourself…"
  "Anybody with half a brain is aware that…"

 Exercise 1

Here are topic sentences for paragraphs. Write a reason that you think will be good support for each topic sentence. Use the method of persuasion that is indicated in brackets.

> **NOTE:**
> – If you cannot think of a specific fact or an example, invent one that supports the topic sentence.
> – Try to find a specific authority, or describe one that would be appropriate for the statement.
>
> **Example:**
> *People should not be able to drive until they are eighteen.*
> *Reason (fact): The Canadian government reports that half the accidents which occur each year involve drivers under the age of eighteen.*

1) People should not be allowed to marry until they are twenty-six years old.
   Reason (fact):

2) Police must be allowed to use Taser guns (전기충격총) and pepper spray to subdue criminals.
Reason (example):

3) Daily exercise is important for good heart health.
Reason (authority):

4) We must ban references to violence in music lyrics.
Reason (predicting the consequence):

 Exercise 2

Read this persuasive paragraph and answer the questions.

      The Canadian government must put a stop to the widespread growth of Casinos and other gambling opportunities. Gambling has become a real problem in Canadian society since gambling venues became easily available to the public. Police Reports in the years 2005 – 2009 indicate that gambling-related crime has risen dramatically. The reports claim too that the types of crime being committed have changed. In 2005, 85% of gambling related crime was reported to be petty theft. In 2009, 65% of gambling related crime included a weapon and in half of these cases, a serious injury occurred. As well, The Canadian Addiction Foundation reports in its June 2010 edition that gambling-related bankruptcies have risen over 500% in the years between 2005 and 2009. These statistics are alarming. And it is not only Casinos that are the problem. For example, lottery tickets are available at most stores and clerks, although required by law to check the age of those purchasing tickets, are not always willing to question a purchaser. This means that children of all ages are beginning to gamble and thus we are increasing the problems that will inevitably result. Not all people gamble foolishly; however, in June of 2011, The Lottery Corporation was pleased to report that the sale of lottery tickets, sports line tickets, and scratch and win tickets is growing each year. This indicates a growing popularity of gambling, and with it comes potential for more crime and personal financial problems. Although the Canadian government makes a great deal of money from the various gambling venues, it must consider the cost in human terms. Gambling is a serious addiction for many and it must be stopped.

1) What method does the writer use in the first reason in his argument?

2) Why would a reader believe the argument?

3) List five arguments used to prove the topic sentence.

4) What statement in the paragraph shows that the writer is trying to argue against a point that might be made in favor of gambling? Underline the sentence.

Exercise 3

Explain why you believe that each of the following arguments is invalid.

Example:
Women with blonde hair are all very gullible. I had a blonde girlfriend who would believe anything anybody told her.
Answer:
Invalid because this is only one single example and since it does not encompass a large enough sample, it is useless.

1) Smoking does not really harm you. Studies made by the Tobacco Companies prove that smoking is harmless.

   Invalid because:

2) Our local car dealer says that they have the lowest prices on new cars in the city.

   Invalid because:

3) Studying has nothing to do with excellent exam results. I never study and I always get good marks.

   Invalid because:

4) Women who go into politics are bad mothers. My father says that he knows a woman in politics who hardly ever sees her family.

Invalid because:

5) If we allow children to chew gum when they are very young, they will never have good teeth when they grow up.

Invalid because

6) People who don't eat meat and dairy products are fools.

Invalid because

7) John should never have been chosen to play on the school baseball team because he dropped the ball twice in the last game.

Invalid because

8) If we get rid of handguns, crime will stop.

Invalid because

9) Anyone who has any feelings at all will oppose hunting.

Invalid because

Transitional Expressions for Argument/Persuasive Paragraphs

Give Reasons:	Answer the Opposition	Draw Conclusions
first (second, third)	of course	therefore
another, next, last, finally	some may say	thus
because, since, for	nevertheless	hence
although	on the other hand	consequently

✏️ Writing Exercise

You are going to write a well-organized five-paragraph essay on one of the following topics. Support and defend your point of view by drawing on your reasoning ability and general experience. Your essay must be 400-600 words in length.

Topics

1. Censorship (신문, 책, 방송등의 검열) is sometimes justified. Do you agree or disagree?

2. High school graduates should take a year off before entering college. Do you agree or disagree?

3. Plastic surgeries: a way to become more beautiful, or someone's unhealthy idea?

4. Should we abandon the concept of "grades" or "marks" in schools?

5. Should parents be permitted to physically punish their children?

ESSAY OUTLINE

Thesis:

Method of Introduction:

Method of Organization (circle one): Time Order, Emphatic Order, Space Order

Three Main Ideas
*First_____
    Examples/Illustrations/Supporting Details
-
-
-

*Second_____
    Examples/Illustrations/Supporting Details
-
-
-

*Third_____
    Examples/Illustrations/Supporting Details
-
-
-

Method of Conclusion:

Lesson 14:
Persuasive/Argumentative Essay – Part 2

> 앞에서 언급한 바와 같이 Persuasive /Argumentative Essay는 TOEFL등의 writing test, 그리고 학교 및 직장에서 가장 흔히 요구되는 essay type입니다. 따라서 지난 lesson에 이어 이번 lesson에도 Persuasive /Argumentative Essay를 공부합니다. 네 가지 strategy와 sample essay들을 공부할 것입니다.

1. Strategies for Argumentation

When you write a Persuasive or Argumentative Essay, you are taking a certain position on a subject and others may not agree with you. You will have to argue your position and convince those whose viewpoint is different from yours that what you have to say is valid. You will need to develop points to prove to your reader that your position on a subject is the correct one.

Here are four techniques that you can use to help you convince your readers.

1-1. Watch Your Language

> 상대방을 비난하는 표현을 삼가합니다. 예를 들어 "Everyone knows…"라는 표현을 쓰면 다른 의견을 가지고 있는 reader를 자기도 모르게 비난하는 결과가 됩니다.

Since you want to win your reader over to your side, it is important not to treat his opinions rudely. You must avoid certain expressions that may anger or annoy the reader. Don't say things like, "Anyone who has a brain will know that…" This kind of statement belittles the reader's intelligence. Also avoid sweeping statements like "Everyone knows…" as the reader may feel that you are disparaging his beliefs.

You must focus on the issue that you are discussing, not on the opinions of those who agree or disagree with you. Keep your writing in the third person. This technique will force you to be objective. Don't write, "My opponents say that communism is a fairer form of government than capitalism." Instead, write, "Supporters of capitalism say that communism takes away individualism." Terms like *my opponents* suggests that others are "bad guys" and such an attitude will create distance between you and your reader. Use words such as "supporters", which are more positive.

1-2. Acknowledge Differing Viewpoints

> 반대의견을 인지하고 있음을 언급함으로써 반대의견도 충분히 고려하였음을 알립니다. 반대의견의 언급은 essay의 시작 부분에 하는 것이 좋습니다.

You cannot simply ignore a point of view that is different or in conflict with yours. By acknowledging other viewpoints, you let the reader know that you have considered the opposing view before coming to your own beliefs. When you think about the opposition's points, you can discern flaws in their argument, and use this to your advantage. One way of acknowledging the opposition is to create a sentence like this:

Although many people believe that it would be financially more sensible for schools to operate all year round, it is important to consider the effect that such a timetable would have on the students and teachers in the system.

Here the writer has acknowledged that one of the main "opposition" issues to maintaining the system as it is now is the fact that financially it would make sense to keep schools operating all year round. The writer has indicated that he or she has thought through the issue, recognizes the popularity of the opposing view, and asks the reader to consider the consequences of the opposition's viewpoint. Readers will likely give more credence to your view if they know you have considered theirs.

If you intend to recognize the opposition's arguments, it is best to do so at the beginning of the essay. In fact, you can use an *"although"* statement as an introduction to your thesis. That way, you have eliminated a strong opposition argument right away, and you have also let your reader know immediately that you have considered another viewpoint.

1-3. Grant the Merits of Differing Viewpoints

> 반대의견에서 타당한 부분이 있으면 이를 알고 있음을 언급합니다.

If an opposing argument is particularly good, then acknowledge it. You will look foolish if you try to deny the validity of a strong argument. You can admit that an opposing argument has merit, but still show the reader that, despite that argument, you still hold your opinion.

1-4. Rebut Differing Viewpoints

반대의견을 반박함으로써 자기의견을 주장합니다.

You have already read about acknowledging your opposition, but sometimes that may not be enough. You may actually have to rebut that opinion; that is, you will need to show where the opinion breaks down. You may have to point out the problems with the opinion.

You can rebut in two ways:

You can first mention all the points raised by the opposition, and then present your counterargument to each of those points.

You can present the first opposition point and present your counterargument to that point. Then you move on to the next point and do the same thing. Then on to the next and so on.

Exercise 1

아래는 서로 상반되는 주장을 하는 두개의 essay입니다. 읽고 질문에 답하세요.

Below are two sample Argumentative Essays written by students. One wants to prove that dangerous sports should be banned and the second one wants to prove that banning is wrong. Read both the essays and then answer the questions that follow them.

Banning Dangerous Sports

Millions of people play sports every day, and, inevitably, some suffer injury or pain. Most players and spectators accept this risk. Dangerous sports should be banned because they lead to violence, participation is not always voluntary and players are at risk of injuries.

      Some sports are nothing but an excuse for violence. Boxing is a perfect example. The last thing an increasingly violent world needs is more violence on our television. The sight of two men (or even women) bleeding, with faces ripped open, trying to obliterate each other is barbaric. Other sports, such as American football or rugby, are also barely concealed violence.

Some people argue that the players can choose to participate. However, this is not always the case. Many boxers, for example, come from disadvantaged backgrounds. They are lured by money or by social or peer pressure and then cannot escape. Even in richer social groups, schools force unwilling students to play aggressive team sports, claiming that playing will improve the students' characters (or the school's reputation), but in fact increasing the risk of injury.

Even when people can choose, they sometimes need to be protected against themselves. Most people approve of governments' efforts to reduce smoking. In the same way, governments need to act if there are unacceptably high levels of injuries in sports such as football, diving, mountaineering, or motor racing.

All sports involve challenge and risk. However, violence and aggression should not be permitted in the name of sport. Governments and individuals must act to limit brutality and violence, so that children and adults can enjoy and benefit from engaging in sports.

Save Our Sports

Today, many sports are becoming increasingly regulated. Boxing, rugby, soccer, and other games are being targeted by sports bodies and medical organizations in an effort to improve safety standards and to reduce injuries. Some people have even campaigned to ban dangerous sports. However, the sports are necessary because they provide valuable social lessons and an outlet for aggression. Also there are the issues of freedom as well as the limitation of the government's power to ban sports.

Sports, competition, and games seem to be natural to humans. Young children learn their own limits and strengths through play with others, but they also learn valuable social lessons about acceptable behavior and the rights of others. Sport therefore is not just a physical phenomenon, but a mental and social one.

Challenging sport provides a healthy, largely safe, physical outlet for aggression. There is very little evidence to show that people who take part in dangerous sports become violent as a result. In fact, it is more likely that apart from the many friendships created in playing, sport acts as a safety valve for a society by reducing stress. Moreover, sport teaches and requires discipline, training, and respect for the rules – valuable lessons in any society.

Almost all sports involve some risk. Young rugby players are paralyzed every year in scrums. Scuba-diving accidents can lead to brain damage or death. Even golf or jogging can lead to pain or injury. Without some elements of risk or challenge, sport becomes meaningless. A marathon runner trying to improve his time, basketball players fiercely battling an opposing team, or a sky-diving team defying gravity – all are trying to push themselves to their maximum. There is therefore no sport without danger.

There is also the issue of freedom. Without a wide range of sports, many people would feel trapped or limited. People should be free to participate in activities with others as long as it does not affect the safety of non-participants.

There also should be limits to the power of governments to ban sports. If one sport is banned because of alleged danger, then what sport would be next? Boxing is the most common target of opponents of dangerous sports. But if boxing is banned, would motor racing follow, then rugby, wrestling, or weightlifting? Furthermore, many sports would go underground, leading to increased injury and illegal gambling. Nobody denies that regulation is needed. Medical bodies have introduced safety rules in boxing, in soccer, and these safety regulations have been welcomed by players. But the role of government should be reduced.

In conclusion, our society would be healthier if more people took part in sports of all kinds. We should continue to try to prevent accidents and injuries. However, we should also ensure that sports are challenging, exciting, and, above all, fun.

1) Which paragraph in Banning Dangerous Sports begins by acknowledging the opposition?

2) In the first body paragraph of Banning Dangerous Sports, what statement is made that requires further explanation? Write the statement.

3) In the third body paragraph of Banning Dangerous Sports, what phrase indicates to the reader that the writer is about to make a comparison?

4) The essay Save Our Sports has more than three body paragraphs. What is the purpose of the third body paragraph?

5) Body paragraphs four and five of Save Our Sports use the same transition. What is it?

6) In the first body paragraph of Save our Sports, where is the topic sentence located?

7) In the second body paragraph of Save Our Sports, what sentence needs to be followed with more supporting detail?

8) What sentence in the fifth body paragraph of Save Our Sports acknowledges the opposition?

9) What method of conclusion is being used in Banning Dangerous Sports?

10) What two words in the concluding paragraph of Save Our Sports should be omitted in the interest of good writing style?

2. Indicating Awareness of the Opposing Opinion

> 반대의견을 인지하고 있음을 언급하는 데는 2가지 경우가 있습니다.
>   1. 반대의견을 생각할 수는 있으나 그 근거를 댈 수 없는 경우
>   2. 반대의견이 실제로 존재함을 알고 있는 경우

Here are two ways of indicating to your reader that you are aware of the opposing opinion

1) When you can think of the opposing opinion but you do not have a specific reference to back up your point, use expressions such as:

   It may be argued (asserted) that……However
   It could be maintained that……However
   It might be said that……However

2) When you have seen the opposing opinion written somewhere, use expressions like:

It has been asserted (argued) that… …However
It is contended (maintained) that… …However
It has been claimed (said) that… …However

 **Exercise 2**

For each of the following issues:

   a. Write a sentence that reflects an opposing opinion.
   b. Write a sentence that states your opinion.
   c. Use the word "however" to introduce your opinion.
   d. Use the suggestions for wording given above. Try to use a different one for each sentence.

Use this example as a guide:
It could be argued that video games prevent children from spending time exercising. However, it has been proven that children who are efficient video game players develop co-ordination that is as good as that learned by playing any sport.

1) Legalizing gambling/casinos

2) Putting drunk drivers in jail

3) Studying abroad

4) Hosting the Olympic Games in a Korean city

 **Exercise 3**

Read the following essay and answer the questions that follow.

Zoos

Children love to go to the zoo. Most of the larger centers in Canada have zoos, and many of them have animals that most people will never see in their natural habitat. Some people feel that imprisonment of animals in these confined areas is cruel punishment, and that zoos should be abolished in favor of allowing the animals to roam in their own environment. However, despite the confined habitat of the zoo, the animal is better off than it would be in the wild. In captivity, there are no predators, diseases are dealt with, and food is always available.

First of all, animals in the wild are always subject to their placement on the food chain. Those lower down like mice, lizards, weasels, rabbits, and snakes supply nourishment for animals larger than themselves. Even larger animals are in danger of being hunted by others. Moose, for example, are huge animals, but they are eaten alive by wolves. Baby giraffe, wildebeest and other plains animals are sought after by members of the cat family. But in the zoo, these animals are protected from others and therefore enjoy a safe life. Statistics prove that animals in zoos live three times as long as those in their natural homes in the wilds.

Another major killer of animals in their own environment is disease. When an animal becomes infected from wounding there are no antibiotics to ease the problem or the pain. Often if an animal is diseased, it will also infect the remaining members of the herd, and thus an entire colony of animal may perish as a result. Disease may also come from the area in which an animal lives. When the natural habitat of an animal is invaded by human industry, the creatures in that area are often affected by air and water pollution from factories. If the animal moves on to other territories, it may take the disease with it. As well as affecting others in the group, it may also pass on its sickness to offspring. The entire species could be weakened by the infection. In zoos, however, sick animals receive immediate attention. The cost of an animal makes medical care compulsory, a protection of investment as much as a caring for the animal itself. For whatever the reason, the animal is well cared for and survival rates are high.

Finally, zoo animals never lack for food. When the natural habitat of an animal is threatened either by human invasion or drought, animals often suffer from starvation. Weak and strong are affected. Even animals that can find some sustenance can be deprived of the required minerals and vitamins that assure their healthy growth. However, in zoos, starvation is a non-issue. Animals are fed good food, in correct portion sizes for the animal and at healthy intervals. Each animal is treated individually, and food is appropriate. The zookeepers are trained to exercise the animals so that they stay healthy.

Living in a zoo is, in many ways, a better life than living in the wilds. Animals are safe from predators, they are treated for disease, and they don't lack food. It is no wonder that animals in the zoo live much longer lives than those in the wild.

1) Write down the thesis statement of the essay.

2) Write down the blueprint of the essay.

3) What sentence in the introductory paragraph of the essay is an acknowledgement of the opposition? Underline the sentence.

4) What word in the introductory paragraph indicates that the writer is going to disprove the opposition point?

5) What transition is used between:

   a. the introductory paragraph and the first body paragraph?

   b. the first and second body paragraphs?

   c. the second and third body paragraphs?

6) What three examples does the writer use to support the topic sentence of the first body paragraph?

7) What method of conclusion is being used by the writer?

8) What sentence in the third body paragraph should be omitted because it does not support the topic sentence?

✎ Writing Exercise

Look at the questions below. You are going to write a well-organized five-paragraph essay on your answer to one of the questions. Support and defend your point of view by drawing on your reasoning ability and general experience. Your essay must be 400-600 words in length.

1. Is a lottery a good idea?

2. We are becoming overwhelmingly dependent on computers. Is this dependence on computers a good thing or should we be more suspicious of their benefits?

3. Should animals be used for scientific research?

4. Should restrictions be placed on the use of mobile phones in public areas like restaurants and subways?

Prewriting

a. Complete the Essay Outline Sheet that is attached to the lesson.

b. In your opening paragraph, acknowledge the opposing point of view before stating your thesis.

c. Remember that you are writing for a reader who probably does not agree with you. Be sure that when you state your opinion, you show reasons why you think the way you do. It isn't enough just to state the opinion.

d. Your concluding paragraph is your final chance to persuade your readers to accept your argument. One of the best ways to end your persuasive essay is to predict what might occur if your opinion is not considered. Try to avoid a mirror ending in this kind of essay. Stimulate your reader by giving him/her the chance to consider the consequences of not acting on your ideas.

Now, write your essay.

ESSAY OUTLINE

Thesis:

Method of Introduction:

Method of Organization (circle one): Time Order, Emphatic Order, Space Order

Three Main Ideas
*First_____

　　Examples/Illustrations/Supporting Details
-
-
-

*Second_____

　　Examples/Illustrations/Supporting Details
-
-
-

*Third_____

　　Examples/Illustrations/Supporting Details
-
-
-

Method of Conclusion:

Lesson 15: Cause and Effect Essay

> 어떤 일의 원인(Cause) 또는 그 일이 어떤 영향을 미치는지(Effect)를 서술하는 Cause and Effect Essay에 대해 공부합니다. Cause and Effect Essay는 학교 및 직장에서 흔히 요구되는 essay type입니다.

Every time something happens, there is at least one cause of the occurrence. As well, every time something happens, there are effects to be dealt with. In these cases, both the causes and effects can be negative or positive.

Every day, we think about why things happen. Why did your best friend quit school? Why did you do so badly on a test? Why did John succeed at a difficult task? What causes colds? We wonder about the causes of these things.

On the other hand, we must also think about the effects of situations and occurrences. What were the effects of your best friend quitting school? What are the effects of success? What are the effects of being the only girl in a family of boys?

The ability to effectively think through causes and effects is a great help in school, employment and in everyday situations.

Most events that are worth exploring have complex causes and effects. They may have several causes, and several effects. Science is constantly dealing with causes and effects. For example, scientists look at diseases and try to determine the causes. They look at possible solutions and try to determine their effects. Doctors investigate the effects of certain medications on their patients. Historians too look at cause and effect. What caused the fall of the Roman Empire and what effect did the fall have on the world of the time?

It is obvious, then, that cause and effect essays involve *analysis*. We must learn to look at a situation, examine it closely, and find more than just the obvious causes.

We must also choose accurate and logical examples of causes and effects. Cause and effect essays make us analyze *why* something happens.

A cause and effect essay may look only at the causes or only at the effects. You will need to do some careful prewriting to discover which pattern you are going to follow.

1. Writing a Cause and Effect Paragraph

Before you write either a cause or effect paragraph, you need to brainstorm both the possible **causes** and **effects** of your topic.

For example, if you want to write a paragraph about a car accident that your friend had you might create lists like the following:

> Causes: Drinking
> Speed
> Lack of attention to the road
> Bad weather conditions
>
> Effects: Driver and passengers hurt badly
> Lost license
> Fined heavily
> Cost of insurance raised
> Car destroyed

In exploring the effects of something, consider both short-term and long-term effects and both negative and positive effects.

1-1. Effect Paragraph

> 어떤 일 또는 사건의 결과 (Effect)를 기술하는 paragraph의 예입니다.

Here is the topic sentence of an **effect** paragraph.

> *According to research, reading to very young children has only positive effects on the child's development.*

1) What is the topic of the paragraph going to be?
   Answer: reading to young children

2) Is the writer going to discuss causes or effects in the paragraph?
   Answer: effects

Words like causes, reasons, and factors are useful to show **causes**. Words like effects, results, and consequences are useful to show **effects**.

 Exercise 1

Here is the entire paragraph:

> According to research, reading to very young children has only positive effects on the child's development. Recent studies in North America have shown that children whose parents read to them on a consistent basis have a better chance of success in school. There are several specific areas that are affected. First of all, a child who has had a parent read to them is not afraid of words. Often children find books terrifying as they cannot fathom the words printed there. However, a child who is read to associates reading with the comfort of home and the kindness and closeness of a parent and as a result, the words are not intimidating. As well, a child who is read to has become familiar with the sounds of words and the creation of correct sentences. These sounds have been repeated over and over in stories told by parents, and often the recognition of the cadence of the sentence and the familiarity of the words make it easier for a child to learn to read by himself. Finally, it has been shown in studies that a child who is read to often follows the words with his or her finger as the parent reads, and by doing so has actually associated letters with sounds, giving him or her a huge advantage when it is time to learn to read in school. Perhaps, on a personal level, the most important immediate result of reading to young children is the joy of sharing time, imagination, and adventure with family. (fathom: 추측하다, 깊이를 재다, cadence: (소리나 말의) 율동적 흐름)

1) How many effects does this writer give for reading to young children? List the effects.

2) Where does the writer claim to have found much of the information?

3) List four transitions used by the writer to move the reader through the ideas.

1-2. Cause Paragraph

> 어떤 일 또는 사건의 원인(Cause)을 기술하는 paragraph의 topic sentence입니다.

Remember that you can also write a paragraph in which you discuss causes. Here is a topic sentence that would introduce a paragraph that will talk about causes.

> *Marriages are not always successful, and it is impossible to list all the reasons why people choose to end their marriages. However, there are three main causes of divorce in North American society.*

1) What is the topic of this paragraph going to be?
    Answer: divorce

2) Will the writer be dealing with the causes or effects of the subject?
    Answer: causes

Types of Causal Relationships

1) A **Necessary Cause** is one that must be present in order to produce a certain effect.
    Example: Gasoline is necessary if the car is going to run.

2) A **Sufficient Cause** is one that can produce an effect without help, although there may be other sufficient causes to produce the same effect.
    Example: Eating too many carbohydrates may make you fat, but lack of exercise may also be a problem.

3) A **Contributory Cause** is one that can help to produce an effect, but cannot do so on its own.
    Example:
    Lack of exercise may lead to being overweight, but eating too much and eating the wrong types of food would also have to be considered. Lots of people don't exercise, yet they are not necessarily fat.

Guidelines for Cause and Effect Paragraph

1) **Don't oversimplify the issues.** If the problem is complex, writing only one single cause is not adequate. Write down as many causes or effects that you can think of. Then choose the three most important causes or effects. By doing this, you will avoid oversimplifying.

2) **Be sure that your list of causes and effects is accurate**. For example, just because two things happen one after another does not mean that they are related. If your mother calls you and at the same time you fall down the stairs, you cannot assume that your mother's call made you fall. Perhaps you were just not looking where you were walking, or you tripped over something that was left on the floor.

3) **Do not confuse causes and effects**. Although this sounds obvious, sometimes separating the two can be tricky. For example, does someone have a good self image because he is successful or is he successful because he has such a good self image?

Transitions and Signal Words in Cause and Effect Writing

Cause and Effect	Degrees of Certainty	Levels of Importance
as a result	certainly	first
because	may	initially
consequently	necessarily	second
due to	perhaps	last
if ... then	possibly	finally
leads to	probably	equally important
therefore	undoubtedly	primarily
thus	unquestionably	above all

 Exercise 2

Each of the following statements contains both a cause and an effect. Write these in the spaces provided after each statement.

Example:

Fewer people are going to hockey games because the tickets are so expensive.
  Cause: *tickets are so expensive*
  Effect: *fewer people are going to hockey games*

1) A tornado was approaching so we ran down into the cellar.

   Cause:
   Effect:

2) Studies have shown that laughter is often the best way to help cure a disease.

   Cause:
   Effect:

3) Many people are asking that schools ban football teams because of the number of severe injuries that young boys suffer in football games.

   Cause:
   Effect:

4) As the use of DVD players is on the rise, the attendance at movie theatres declines.

   Cause:
   Effect:

5) According to sports coaches, great players develop as a result of dedication and hard work.

   Cause:
   Effect:

Writing Exercise - Paragraphs

Writing #1

You are going to write a paragraph which deals with **causes**. Your paragraph must be 125-150 words in length. Choose one of the following topics and use one of the attached Paragraph Planning Sheets to help you organize your work.

Topics:
1. Causes of violence in schools
2. Reasons for success in business
3. Reasons why some people cheat at school

Writing #2

You are going to write a paragraph which deals with **effects**. Your paragraph must be 125-150 words in length. Choose one of the following topics and use one of the attached Paragraph Planning Sheets to help you organize your work.

Topics:
1. The effects of prejudice
2. The effects of drug abuse
3. The effects of cheating at school

Paragraph Planning Sheet

Topic:

Narrowed topic:

Controlling Idea:

Topic Sentence:

List of **causes or effects** to support the topic sentence: (List as many as you can think of and then eliminate all but **three or four** of the strongest points)

1.

2.

3.

4.

5.

6.

7.

8.

Concluding Idea:

Paragraph Planning Sheet

Topic:

Narrowed topic:

Controlling Idea:

Topic Sentence:

List of **causes or effects** to support the topic sentence: (List as many as you can think of and then eliminate all but **three or four** of the strongest points)

1.
2.
3.
4.
5.
6.
7.
8.

Concluding Idea:

2. Developing a Cause and Effect Essay

When you are planning a Cause and Effect Essay, you need to brainstorm the event that you want to write about. Depending on your topic, you may want to do some research.

Think very carefully about details that you have listed in your brainstorming. Check to be sure that your conclusions are valid. You must be able to prove the cause-effect relationships you have suggested.

Ask yourself, for each cause-effect relationship:
1) Am I sure that there is a cause and effect relationship here?
2) Have I neglected to consider other possibilities?
3) Have I assumed that there is a cause and effect relationship between two events just because they follow each other?
4) Have I made a distinction between a long-term and short-term cause or effect? A short-term cause or effect is a single, immediately identifiable event. A long-term cause or effect may be less easy to pinpoint but in the long run more important.
5) Have I distinguished between the most important effects and those that are less significant?

As you write, you may also consider asking yourself the following questions:
1) Who was responsible? That is, who caused the problem?
2) Who was impacted? That is, who was affected?
3) What consequences did the event have on a broader economic or social scale?

 Exercise 3

The following is a cause and effect essay written by a student. Read it carefully and answer the questions that follow it.

The Rise of Divorce Rates

From the past to the present, people all over the world have determined to live together in some type of "marriage" relationship. In the past, a commitment to a "marriage" has meant that the partners do truly adhere to their vows – that is, they stay together despite bad times. However, more recently, couples who are having difficulty maintaining their relationships are turning to divorce. Divorce rates are higher than ever before. But why? The modern world has brought new problems for marriages. The role of women in society has changed; there is greater stress at home and in the workplace; and communication has become a thing of the past.

The role of women has changed in recent times. In the past, men have been relied on to provide for their families, and women stayed at home to care for the house and the children. A "housewife" who had no money of her own and was dependent on her husband had no way to leave a troubled marriage. However today, women work in positions that pay well and provide them with an independent income. As a result, they are more able to end a bad marriage and still find it possible to cope financially on their own. As well, in the past, many women were confined to their homes. Families had only one car, and thus the woman was often housebound while her husband took the car to work. With only herself, her children and her neighbors to communicate with, she often lived an unworldly existence. Women used to visit their neighbors for coffee in the mornings. Now women are out in the workforce and they have the opportunity to experience the world around them. This may result in a desire to break free from a marriage and explore the other options that the world presents.

Another cause of rising divorce rates comes from the increasing stress of modern life. Good jobs are difficult to get and single salaries are not sufficient to support a family anymore. Homes, cars, appliances, food, and clothing are expensive. Also, tuition fees at universities are skyrocketing. As a result, couples often have trouble making ends meet. There may be fights about money – how it should be spent, what should be saved – and the stress is often too much for a marriage. Furthermore, the stress of finances does not end with retirement. Often people do not have pension plans, and government pensions are far too small to support a retirement. A growing number of older, long-married couples are divorcing these days, many as a result of the stress of retirement finances. Financial pressure is one of the leading causes of divorce in Canada today.

The most significant cause of divorce is simple – lack of communication. Given that women are working outside the home, and both husband and wife may be focused on their jobs, communication between the two is sometimes lacking. Problems that develop within the marriage are never really dealt with because both parties are so busy. After a hard day at work, it is often easier for couples to ignore their difficulties rather than make the day worse by discussing them. Things then begin to build up to a breaking point, and often come to a place where there is nothing that can be done to fix the situation. Another communication problem comes from the development of technology. The television, the DVD player, the computer and the video games are popular methods of entertainment in this age. As a result, people have a tendency not to talk, but rather spend their leisure in electronic pastimes. People stop talking to each other and then find that they don't know the other person anymore. Divorce may not be a big step, since the couple rarely spends time together anyway.

The concept of family is still important in society. However, people are finding it more difficult to remain in marriage situations that are not happy or loving. Our modern world has changed the way people view and experience marriage, and thus divorce rates are on the rise.

1) Write the sentence in the first body paragraph that should be omitted in the interest of paragraph unity.

2) What is the thesis statement of this essay?

3) What are the three main ideas that the writer is going to discuss in the essay?

4) What is the focus of this Cause and Effect Essay – the causes, or the effects?

5) List two transitions used by the writer in the second body paragraph.

6) What are the two main examples given by the author in the third body paragraph of the essay?

 Exercise 4

Each of the following statements requires either causes or effects. Provide three separate causes or three separate effects for each of the following statements.

Example:
Many children are afraid of the dark
    Effects: 1. They want to sleep with a light on.
                 2. They want to sleep in their parents' room.
                 3. They want to have a parent stay with them until they go to sleep.

1) Hunting is not considered to be acceptable any more.

2) University graduates tend to marry and have families later than high school graduates.

3) Rugby should not be allowed as a high school sport.

4) University tuition should be free.

5) People should not be allowed to have a driver's license until they are twenty.

Writing Exercise

Now that you have written the outlines (causes or effects) in the Exercise 4 above, decide which one you will use to write your essay. You are to write a well-organized five-paragraph essay based on the ideas you developed in the exercise. Your essay must be 400-600 words in length.

Here are some ideas for your prewriting

a. Look at your outline above.
   - The statement is your thesis.
   - The three main causes or effects that you have listed will be your three main ideas.
   - Make sure that your three ideas are really separate from each other and that they are not restatements of each other. Make sure that they do not overlap.
   - Make sure that they are really "causes" or "effects", not simply chronological developments before and after the situation.

b. Decide whether you will use several examples to support each of the main ideas or whether you will use one extended example.

c. List as many details as you can to help you make your decision. Use the attached Essay Outline Sheet to help you organize your work.

ESSAY OUTLINE

Thesis:

Method of Introduction:

Method of Organization (circle one): Time Order, Emphatic Order, Space Order

Three Main Ideas
*First_____

<u>Examples/Illustrations/Supporting Details</u>

-
-
-

*Second_____

<u>Examples/Illustrations/Supporting Details</u>

-
-
-

*Third_____

<u>Examples/Illustrations/Supporting Details</u>

-
-
-

Method of Conclusion:

Lesson 16: Definition Essay

> 어떤 사물 또는 용어에 대해 개념을 설명하는 Definition Essay에 대해 공부합니다.

Often when we talk to people, we use words or expressions that may need to be explained. For example: "I think that my brother is miserable". I might explain what I mean by "miserable" by saying that he is always in a bad mood. When he was at dinner last night, he complained about everything on his plate even though my mother had worked hard to make a meal to please him.

Often a word or phrase will mean one thing to one person and something different to someone else. In order to understand each other, we need to clarify the meaning of the word or phrase that we are dealing with. Definition writing states the literal meaning of a word or phrase; definitions set the boundaries around meanings.

A Definition Essay is designed to explain and clarify with examples. In a definition essay, the writer explains his/her understanding of a concept, expressed as a word or phrase. The meaning is illustrated to the reader through a series of examples and illustrations.

As with any essay, a definition essay takes advantage of many of the methods of development that you have learned about. Narration, description, examples and illustrations should be used by the writer to provide explanations of the concept that you are writing about.

Learning to define your terms is a basic communication skill. The clearer you are, the more your reader will understand your writing.

Definition essays should be personal since they are defining your ideas about a concept. They should also be dynamic, inspiring, perhaps amusing, and certainly memorable.

When you choose a topic, try to keep it broad. Don't choose something so specific that there is no leeway for interpretation.

1. Types of Definition

> 사물을 define하는 7가지 방법에 대해 공부합니다.

There are many types of definitions that you can use in a definition essay. All of these methods are used to clarify meaning for your reader.

1-1. Analysis

> 대상을 세분하여 각 부분에 대해 각각 설명하는 방법

You may choose to write about a subject that can be divided into several parts. Divide it up and then define each part separately.

Example:
"A triathlon is a type of race that involves three separate events: swimming, running, and bicycling."
The writer would continue by defining and describing each part.

1-2. Classification:

> 먼저 대상을 큰 category로 분류한 후 그 category 안에서 다시 define하는 방법

This type of definition is often required in formal writing and reports. There are two parts to this type of definition:

- First, the word needs to be placed in the larger category or class to which it belongs.

    Example:
    A biography is a type of writing…
    An evergreen is a tree…

- Next, the writer must give details or characteristics which distinguish this word from others in its category or class.

    Example:
    A biography is a type of writing that is about someone's life.
    An evergreen is a tree with needles that it keeps all year round.

When you write a class definition, be sure that the class is not too large to begin with.

> **Example:**
> *An evergreen is a plant…*

This is too vague, and it will make it difficult for you to pinpoint a distinguishing detail. As well, try to make your distinguishing fact as specific as you can.

> **Example:**
> *An evergreen is a tree that has needles.*

Saying that the evergreen has needles does not distinguish it from the trees which drop needles every winter. It is simply not specific enough to give your reader a good clear picture.

1-3. Comparison:

> 잘 알지 못하는 사물을 잘 아는 사물과 비교하여 설명하는 방법

You can define something that is unfamiliar to the reader by comparing it to something with which the reader is familiar. This technique is used by writers and poets whenever they employ similes (직유법), metaphors (은유법) and personification (의인법).

> **Example:**
> A tiger is an enormous cat.
> A flashbulb memory is a picture captured forever in the brain.

1-4. Details:

> 사물의 특성이나 구별되는 속성을 설명하는 방법

You can define something by describing its physical characteristics and distinguishing attributes.

> **Example:**
> *A defining moment* can be described as an occurrence in life that changes the way someone behaves or reacts in the future.

1-5. Examples and Incidents:

> 예를 들어 define하는 방법

You can define something by giving examples and illustrations.

Example:
Dad's photographic memory gave him an advantage when he was in school since he could visualize the words on every page that he had read.

1-6. Negation:

> Define하고자 하는 사물에 대해 먼저 "기존의 개념"을 부인한 후 그 사물에 대해 "새로운 개념"을 설명하는 방법

In this type of definition, the writer actually states what something is not, and then says what it is.

Example:
A good friend does not just support and understand you, but also is honest and firm when necessary.

University is not just a place for book learning but a place for social and emotional development.

This technique is very useful when you know that your reader already has his own idea about a word or phrase. You approach him by telling him that the word does not mean what he believes, but rather means something else entirely.

1-7. Results, Effects, and Uses:

> 사물의 결과, 용도를 설명하며 define하는 방법

You can define the subject by stating the consequences and uses of it.

Example:
Gaining self-confidence will ensure that a person becomes stronger and more able to deal with life.

 **Exercise 1**

Read the following definition essay and answer the questions.

Heroes

When you hear the word "hero", what picture comes to mind? Most likely, you will see a man, tall, daring, probably handsome, and most often young and athletic. He may be the "knight in shining armor", the strongman who slays fire-eating dragons. But these characteristics are really the stuff of legends and tales of adventure. In our society, heroes come in all shapes and sizes, and they are more realistic than those of the ancient fairytales and legends.

Although the Merriam-Webster dictionary defines a hero as "a mythological or legendary figure often of divine descent endowed with great strength or ability; an illustrious warrior; a man admired for his achievements and noble qualities or one that shows great courage", society's accepted definition of the word is much broader. In fact, today, we recognize different types of heroes.

One strong tradition of the hero is found in the early tales of the Greeks. Their heroes, all male, followed a specific pattern in their lives. With a "god" as a father, and a quest set out for life, they battled mythological creatures, saved lives, and destroyed evil with strength of mind and body, albeit with the help of magic and a woman. They succeeded in their quests and were rewarded with kingships and power.

These Greek heroes became the forerunners of the heroes of literature. Like the Greeks, more modern writers focused on the male as the main character in a story. For the most part, this new hero became more realistic in that he no longer had an attachment to the "gods", magic, or the dragons of his predecessor. But the heroes were still mostly males and until the mid-1900s women did not often appear as the heroes of novels. However, the women's movements of the last century promoted women protagonists with whom females could relate in a positive manner. They have been successful. Literature has sprouted a large number of famous female protagonists created by both male and female authors.

But the word hero is now applied to a broader base than simply literature. Today's society uses the word "hero" frequently. A hero can save a life. A hero can foil a robbery. A hero can donate a million dollars to find a cure for cancer. A hero can score the winning goal in a hockey game. A hero can climb a tree and retrieve a frightened cat. All these are heroes to someone, although the deed may be big or small.

It seems, then, that heroes are personalized these days and are identified according to our own needs. If a young child yearns to be a famous sports star, he or she may find a "hero" in the sports field who represents to the child everything he or she wants to become. If a woman is overweight and sees the success that someone else has had in losing weight, then that woman may see the other as a hero – someone worth emulating. In these cases, the hero has become a role model for behavior.

But what is the common thread in heroism? In many cases, there is often a sacrifice of the hero's personal safety. There may be danger involved in heroism. The hero who saves a life may put his or her own in jeopardy. The hero who stops a robbery may find himself or herself in the line of fire. Even the hero who climbs a tree to save a cat may face the possibility of falling or being scratched for his or her efforts. A hero is selfless, putting the needs of someone else before his or her own.

As well, a true hero does not recognize his or her actions as heroic. Because true heroes are selfless, they do not need the accolades of heroism. They avoid public recognition of their deeds. True heroism is action without thought of reward.

So heroes do not have to accomplish earth-shattering deeds. In fact, they are simply people whose selflessness, courage, and concern for others make them special to those whose lives they affect.

1) What method of introduction is used?

2) What is the purpose of the conclusion in "Heroes"?

3) What type of definition is being used in the following passages?

   a. *Heroes do not have to accomplish earth-shattering deeds.*

   b. *Although the Merriam-Webster dictionary defines a hero as "a mythological or legendary figure often of divine descent endowed with great strength or ability; an illustrious warrior; a man admired for his achievements and noble qualities or one that shows great courage", society's accepted definition of the word is much more broad.*

4) What type of definition is being used in the third and fourth paragraph?

5) In the fifth paragraph, what method is the author using to define the term?

 **Exercise 2**

Read the following definition essay and answer the questions.

Love

According to a famous movie, "Love means never having to say you're sorry." Or does it? There have been songs sung about love, books written about it, studies conducted about it, and wars fought over it. Despite the fact that most of us have experienced a feeling that we explain as "love", when we are asked to define the emotion, we all have different things to say. Perhaps this is because "love" is a personal experience, and our definition of it depends on who we are as individuals and how we relate to the world around us. So, in order to define "love", we need to look not only at what it is, but at what it is not. As well, we need to recognize that there are different types of love.

What is "love"? For some, it is the touch of a hand on a summer evening walk. It may be the warmth of a hug to ease distress or pain. Or perhaps it is the sound of a snore in the bed at night, assuring us that someone we know is there in the darkness. It may be the reassuring smile across a room filled with strangers, or the thrill of a whispered "I love you" when you least expect it. Love is that feeling that fills your body with the knowledge that you are not alone and that you are special. However, there are dangers that exist in the closeness of "love".

The marriage ceremony tells couples that they are now "one", and too often people interpret this as meaning that they must always be attached. They never go out alone; they spend their time only on pursuits in which they both participate; they eat only the food that the two of them like; and they form friendships only with people they both enjoy. However, this is not "love". Love does not mean that people must lose their individuality. It does not mean that the lovers must give up activities that they enjoy. No, loving someone means accepting differences, and in fact, enjoying them. Each partner brings something different to a relationship, and to deny this uniqueness is to reject those very things that created the love in the first place. The "adhesive tape" kind of love is often born of jealousy and mistrust, and these characteristics have no place in honest commitment.

But when we talk of love, we tend to focus on the romantic form of the emotion. Unfortunately, in our society, we use the word "love" to apply to many things. A girl will "love" her new pair of shoes, a boy will "love" his new hockey stick, a mother will "love" the break from the chores, a critic will "love" a new movie. However, are these true examples of love? Not really. There are different types of love, but in the true sense of the word, they apply to human relationships with other living things. A parent loves a child and, despite difficulties, the love is unconditional. A child loves his dog and curls up to sleep with it at night; a brother loves his sister and comes to her defense when she is threatened; a man loves his mother and weeps when she is gone. These are true feelings of love and they come from deep within the self.

Love may be hard to define, but it is easy to feel. It evokes the emotions – from joy to rage. The feeling is defined by our own view of the world, and the way we react to others; it is as individual as DNA, and it is ours to enjoy.

1) What method of introduction is used in this essay?

2) What three ideas does the writer of "Love" intend to discuss in the essay?

3) What types of definitions are being used in the following sentences?

    a. For some, it is the touch of a hand on a summer evening walk.

    b. Love does not mean that people must lose their individuality.

4) Identify the transition between the second and third paragraphs of the essay.

5) How many examples does the writer use in the second paragraph of the essay?

Writing Exercise

Below you will find a list of types of people with whom we come into contact during our lives. Choose one of them and write a five-paragraph definition essay explaining what that term means to you. Your essay must be 400-600 words in length.

- Snob
- Loser
- Bully
- Optimist
- Pessimist
- Slob
- Loner
- Hypocrite
- Cheapskate
- Busybody
- Whiner

Prewriting Strategies

a. First of all, find the definition of the word in the dictionary. If there are several meanings for the word, you need to choose one. Don't introduce your essay with the statement, "According to the dictionary, the word…" This beginning is overused!

b. Remember that the thesis of a definition essay must tell the reader what the term means to you!

c. When you plan your supporting paragraphs, you should consider three aspects of the term that you have chosen. Each paragraph will discuss one of these aspects.

d. Support each paragraph with several examples or a single extended example.

ESSAY OUTLINE

Thesis:

Method of Introduction:

Method of Organization (circle one): Time Order, Emphatic Order, Space Order

Three Main Ideas
*First_____

    Examples/Illustrations/Supporting Details

-
-
-

*Second_____

    Examples/Illustrations/Supporting Details

-
-
-

*Third_____

    Examples/Illustrations/Supporting Details

-
-
-

Method of Conclusion:

Lesson 17: Division and Classification Essay

> Division and Classification Essay는 사물을 분류하고 카테고리 별로 구분하는 방식으로 전개해 나가는 essay입니다.

1. What is Classification?

What is the purpose of a division or classification essay? The purpose is to give readers a new way of looking at things, often in an entertaining and humorous way.

For students, learning the techniques of division and classification can reap excellent rewards. Doing well on essay assignments often depends on the student's ability to classify. Exams and reports also require classification skills; tests in Literature, Science, and History may require you to classify before you write your answer.

Classification is especially helpful in organizing large groups of ideas into smaller recognizable divisions.

For example, you may be asked to do something like the following:
"Explain the reasons for the fall of the Roman Empire."

You would start by listing the causes, then **classifying** them into groups of similar or related causes. By doing this you would be **dividing** the large topic into smaller pieces. If you wrote about all the causes without classifying them, you would have a disorganized essay.

Thus, after listing the causes of the "fall of the Roman Empire", the next step is to classify the causes – that is, place them into categories. Perhaps as you read the list of causes you have thought of, you might see that they fall into three categories: Social, Economic, and Political. Once you have classified the items, you have the materials for three strong paragraphs to support your thesis. By taking the ideas that you listed and placing them under the appropriate category, you will have the details for the paragraph on that particular category.

Dividing and classifying in our writing allows us to sort out the information that we receive. We break down large, complex subjects into smaller, more manageable categories.

– The choice of categories or classifications of your ideas will depend on what purpose you have for your writing.
– Then, you must decide which way you want to organize or divide your ideas according to the classifications you have chosen.

Division and Classification essays require you to choose a reason to classify your subject, or a classifying principle which suits your audience and your purpose.

For example, if you were writing about vehicles, you might want to sort them out into the following three different categories:

Category A	Category B	Category C
Sedans	Economy Cars	Cars for youth
Vans	Luxury cars	Cars fir families
Trucks	Environ-friendly cars	Cars for old folks

1) If you chose category A, you might be writing for someone who does not know much about vehicles and your purpose would be to teach them about the different types of vehicles available, according to their size and use.

2) If you chose category B, you might be writing for someone who is interested in the relative costs of vehicles and your purpose would be to help them understand the cost advantages and disadvantages of each.

3) If you chose category C, you might be writing to explain to someone that different age groups enjoy or need different types of vehicles.

So you can see that the division and classification of ideas must depend on the purpose of your writing and the audience for which it is intended.

Division and Classification activities will be part of your education, not only in essay writing, but also for reports in most other subjects.

2. Guidelines for Division/Classification Essay

1) **Do not try to write about a subject that has too many classes.** You don't want to have a class called "Miscellaneous", since you will have a number of potentially unrelated ideas in the category, and writing a topic sentence to represent all of them will be virtually impossible.

Example:
An essay classifying languages would be far too long – you would need to write a book instead. However, an essay classifying languages spoken in a certain country would be easier to accomplish.

2) **Choose a single unifying principle for classifying your thoughts.**

   Example:
   If you have a long list of things to buy when you go out on Saturday morning, then perhaps you should classify the list according to the store where each item is to be purchased. You could use the following classifications:

   department store items
   grocery store items
   drug store items

Or, you might classify them on the basis of their importance. If you don't have a lot of money available, you could use the following list:

necessary items
items needed in the future
extra items that I don't really need

How a topic is divided up depends on the purpose of the writer and the audience for whom the writing is intended. However, in order for the writing to be clear and consistent, the classification should be made according to a **single unifying principle**. This means that once you have selected a principle for making your division, you can concentrate exclusively on developing the categories that come from it. In the first case above, the division was made based on the principle of **item type**. The second division was made on the principle of **importance of item**. Different classifications can apply at different times to the same subject, but it is essential that you use only one dividing principle at a time.

   Example:
   Vehicles can be classified by price. They can also be classified by brand name, style, use, and reliability. Choose the one principle of classification suitable to your purpose.

   Look at the following classifications:
   Fords, Hondas, Trucks

The classifications are not consistent. The first two are brands of cars, and the third category relates to the style of vehicle.

Here is another example:
Italian food, Greek food, Thai food, pizza

The classifications are not consistent here either. In fact, the details of your essay may overlap. When you discuss Italian food, you are most likely going to talk about pizza, so having pizza as one of the categories will lead to a repetition of ideas.

So, be sure you divide your subject into separate and distinct categories according to a single unifying principle.

3) **Try to develop your categories equally.** You should write the same amount for each category. Keep your paragraphs equal in length, and give each category the same number of details.

4) **Develop each category completely.** Think carefully about your details and make sure that you have included all of the significant elements of each category. Don't leave things out! Your reader will be quick to see any loopholes in your discussion.

5) **Be sure to use enough examples to make each category distinct from the others.** Also, you need to ensure that all individual aspects of your subject fit into one of the categories (classes) that you have devised. For example, classifying teachers as good or bad is not going to cover those who are mediocre (보통의, 평범한). You will need another category to deal with that group.

Review:
- Divide the subject into major categories that have some common trait.
- Subdivide those categories into smaller parts. Be sure that your classification system is consistent.
- Ensure that each category has the same unifying principle.
- Make sure that the categories are complete, logical and equal, and that you have not left out any details.

 Exercise 1

Classify each of the following topics in TWO different ways.

Example:
Topic: Television Shows
Categories:
        a) Drama
           Comedy
           Reality Shows

        b) Shows on NBC
           Shows on ABC
           Shows on the Fox network

In a) the shows have been classified by type, and in b) they have been classified by the network on which they appear.

1) Friends
    a)

    b)

2) Shopping
    a)

    b)

3) Music
    a)

    b)

4) Hobbies
   a)

   b)

5) Food
   a)

   b)

 **Exercise 2**

Here is a sample Division/Classification Essay. Read it carefully and answer the questions that follow it.

Rehabilitative Therapies

When many people hear the word "therapy," they think of something that has caused a problem and has to be fixed. In most cases, that is true. Most people think the problem may be an injury that has to be rehabilitated or an extreme mental problem for which the person needs serious help. However, therapy does not always deal with injured or mentally troubled people. Three types of therapy that help a wide range of people with their problems are physical, occupational, and speech therapies.

Physical therapy is the type that deals mostly with injuries and their rehabilitation. According to the *Occupational Outlook Handbook*, "Physical therapists provide services that help restore function, improve mobility, relieve pain, and prevent or limit permanent physical disabilities of patients suffering from injuries or disease". Disabling conditions such as lower-back pain, cerebral palsy (뇌성마비), arthritis (관절염), heart disease, and fractures (골절), as well as physical injuries, are among the cases physical therapists often evaluate and treat. This therapy often includes strength-building exercises. Therapists in this field work on the person's flexibility, endurance, strength, balance, and coordination. Most therapy is done in specialized clinics or hospitals by a licensed physical therapist who has a bachelor's degree.

Physical therapy is a fairly new practice of rehabilitation. The treatments were not widely practiced until after World War I, when soldiers returned home with injuries that were able to be rehabilitated by this therapy. The profession immediately began to grow and has been popular in the U.S. since that time. The vocation is also expected to continue growing for several more years. But physical therapy is not the only type of therapy that addresses the rehabilitation of injuries.

The other therapy type that may deal with some injuries is occupational therapy, or "OT" as it is often called for short. Enhancing fine motor skills(정교한 운동기능) is the focus of OT. Occupational therapists set goals for their patients that will enable them to have more "independent, productive, and satisfying lives," by teaching them how to perform daily functions without the aid of others. Some of these activities may include eating, getting dressed, or using the bathroom. Exercises that improve balance, coordination, trunk control (몸통조절능력), dexterity (손동작조절능력), and basic muscle movement are used to enhance a person's progress toward an easier lifestyle. Occupational therapists work mainly with people who have disabilities. These may include people with spinal cord injuries, cerebral palsy, muscular dystrophy (근이영양증: 근육이 퇴화하는 질병), or people who have had a stroke.

Occupational therapy is my current major of study, so I am doing volunteer work for several therapists right now at Parent-Child Services in West Knoxville. It is very interesting to sit and observe each session. I am presently observing a four-year-old victim of near drowning who was thought to be dead, but was brought back to life. His focus is on balance and coordination right now. I am also observing a child with cerebral palsy, and he is one of my favorite children to work with. He is working on strengthening his muscles in his trunk and legs while continuing to develop better balance and coordination. Most patients, such as these, are treated with OT in clinics, hospitals, or schools. An occupational therapist must have a bachelor's degree and be licensed by the state in order to practice.

As well as physical and occupational therapy, speech therapy is another type of treatment that addresses some disabilities and injuries. Speech therapy is usually grouped with the other two types but is not as involved with physical injury. Speech-language pathologists (언어병리학자) and audiologists (청능사) help people who have speech and hearing defects. They identify the problem, and then use tests to further evaluate it. Speech-language pathologists and audiologists also try to improve the speech and hearing defect through a variety of treatments. These therapists also treat patients with communication, voice, or swallowing problems. The person's problem may be a result of hearing loss, brain deterioration, stroke, or mental retardation (정신지체). Speech therapists help a person with pronouncing words, making sounds, or controlling pitch. For those who are hearing impaired, therapists may teach them sign language to help them better communicate with others. A great deal of this type of therapy takes place in specialized clinics while some speech therapists work in schools, teaching children how to relate to others. All licensed speech therapists are required to have a master's degree to practice ("Speech").

These three types of therapy – physical, occupational, and speech – are just a few that are offered to those with disabilities or injuries. Even though they are very different in their realms of patients, problems, and solutions, the main goal of each therapist is to work with patients to help them recover and live easier lifestyles. Some people cannot fully recover, but all the help they can receive is a step forward. These therapies have been very beneficial to an abundance of people over the years, and the job market for these services is continually growing as more and more people are beginning to need such treatments. The outlook for therapists in these fields looks good as employment is expected to increase at a rate faster than average through 2008.

Questions:

1) What is the thesis statement in the essay?

2) What word in the thesis statement indicates that the writer has acknowledged the opposing viewpoint?

3) What three categories has the writer used to classify the information for the essay?

4) How has the writer made a transition from the first category to the second?

5) The writer has used two paragraphs to discuss the first category. What is the main idea in each paragraph?

6) What transition word does the writer use in the first sentence of the second category to tie the two categories together?

7) The writer has divided the information for the second category into two paragraphs. What is the purpose of each paragraph?

8) How does the writer transition to the third category?

9) What two techniques does the writer use in the concluding paragraph of the essay?

✏ Writing Exercise

You are going to write a five-paragraph Division and Classification Essay on one of the following topics. Your essay must be 400-600 words in length.

Choose a topic and then follow the Prewriting steps listed below.

Friends	Shopping
Music	Hobbies
Books	Television shows
Pets	Food

Prewriting

1) Write down all the ideas that you have for your topic. Write without worrying about spelling or grammar. Don't be concerned if the ideas sound silly. Just get all your ideas down on paper.

2) Divide your ideas up into three categories. Be sure that the categories are all distinct and different from each other. Try to keep them evenly divided. You may want to try to categorize the ideas in several different ways to find the best division. When you are satisfied with your classification, then you can discard ideas that don't fit into any category.

3) Complete the Essay Outline Sheet that is attached to the lesson.

4) Write your essay.

ESSAY OUTLINE

Thesis:

Method of Introduction:

Method of Organization (circle one): Time Order, Emphatic Order, Space Order

Three Main Ideas
*First_____

    Examples/Illustrations/Supporting Details

-
-
-

*Second_____

    Examples/Illustrations/Supporting Details

-
-
-

*Third_____

    Examples/Illustrations/Supporting Details

-
-
-

Method of Conclusion:

Lesson 18:
Comparison and Contrast Essay

> Comparison and Contrast Essay는 사물을 비교하고 대조하는 기법의 essay 입니다. 두 사물의 비슷한 점 (compare)과 다른 점 (contrast)을 분석하여 사물에 대한 명확한 이해와 올바른 결론을 유도하는 writing은 학교 및 직장에서 흔히 요구됩니다.

We are constantly comparing and contrasting in our daily lives. We compare and contrast many things – for example, different types of cold medicines, brands of athletic shoes, or fast food outlets. When we shop for cars, we compare different types of vehicles by looking at their similarities and their differences.

When we **compare**, we are looking at the similarities between things. When we **contrast**, we are looking at the *differences* between things.

The purpose of comparing and contrasting is to help us understand the two things more clearly, and this understanding helps us to make decisions and judgments about them.

Comparison and contrast essays begin with thoughts about how things are the same and how they differ. The essay takes some items which have a common basis (e.g., types of cars) and then uses analysis to break down the ideas into sections which show the points of sameness or of difference. The essay uses examples to make the similarities (comparison) or differences (contrast) clear to the reader.

During our lives, we learn new things by comparing them with things that we already understand. For example:

> *Mr. Taylor is my new history teacher. I want to tell my friend about Mr. Taylor's abilities as a teacher. We both know another teacher, Mrs. Brown, and we are aware of her methods, so I describe Mr. Taylor by describing how his methods are* **similar** *to Mrs. Brown's and how they are* **different**.
>
> *My friend may make a judgment about Mr. Taylor based on the information that I have given. She might also make a decision either to try to get into Mr. Taylor's class or to avoid him as a teacher.*

In the same way, **comparison** essays may be designed to **inform** readers of new material by showing the similarities between familiar ideas, people, or issues, and unfamiliar or seemingly dissimilar concepts.

Essays that **contrast** different ideas may sometimes be designed to **persuade** readers to think about the differences between two points and choose a side in the discussion.

Both types of essays lead to judgments or decisions.

The ability to compare and contrast is useful both in writing for school and in the workplace.
At school, you may be asked to compare the themes of two books, the causes of two major wars, or the features of two types of computer programs. At work, you may be required to evaluate two ways of doing something in the office, two choices of new equipment, or two methods of shipping materials. In all cases, you will need to analyze the pros and cons of each choice – that is, compare and contrast the two.

The comparison/contrast essay allows you to really look closely at things. You may find that you see things that you haven't seen before, and that you are paying more attention to details before you draw a conclusion. You may start to see more complex relationships between things. And in your daily life, you will find that the skills of comparison and contrast help you in making good decisions.

1. Contrast Paragraph

> 두 사물의 서로 다른 점을 분석하는 Contrast Paragraph에 대해 공부합니다.

Here is the topic sentence of a contrast paragraph:

> *There are two different ways to discipline children – one promotes physical punishment and one that promotes reason.*

The writer begins a contrast paragraph with a topic sentence that clearly states what two persons, things, or ideas will be contrasted.

1-1. One Side at a Time

> 위의 topic sentence에 대한 paragraph입니다. "One side at a time" 방식으로 대조 (contrast) 한 paragraph입니다.

Here is the entire paragraph. Read it and answer the questions which follow.

There are two different ways to discipline children – one promotes physical punishment and one that promotes reason. Physical punishment is practiced by some parents who believe that a little bit of discomfort will deter children from repeating an unacceptable action. Parents will slap a child's hand if he touches something forbidden, or pat a child's bottom if he behaves badly. Parents who believe in this method of discipline state that a child, in a dangerous situation, will respond quickly to a sharp tap on the hand, bottom or leg. They feel that the instant reaction may actually keep a child safe. The danger of course is that the parent will forget his or her own strength and hit the child too hard. There is a fine line between physical discipline and abuse. On the other hand, some parents believe that reasoning with a child is the best method of discipline. They do not believe that a child should be hit at any time. If a child misbehaves, the parent in this case will talk to the child and get him to understand why his behavior is not appropriate. Children learn to understand the reasons why parents are not pleased with them, and they will then stop before they do the same thing another time, and this thinking process will keep them safe from harm. In the 'reasoning' method, there is no danger that a child will be harmed physically as at no time will the parent impose his strength on the child, however, a child may not learn immediately and thus his behavior might be repeated. There are certainly advantages to both methods of discipline; however, recent studies seem to indicate that a child who is physically disciplined may mimic the parent and use similar tactics when dealing with others.

 ## Exercise 1

1) What are the two things being compared and contrasted in the paragraph?

2) What is positive about physical discipline?

3) What is negative about physical discipline?

4) Which type of discipline is discussed first?

5) What final point does the writer make?

6) What do you notice about the organization of the paragraph?

7) What transition has been used to get from a discussion of one type of discipline to the other?

Before composing the paragraph, the writer probably brainstormed or freewrote to gather ideas and then made an outline like this:

Points of Contrast	Physical	Reason
1. communication	hitting	talk
2. effectiveness	instant reaction	longer time to react
3. dangers	mimicked behavior parent hits too hard	reaction is not immediate child may not learn the first time

If you organize your paragraph in this way, you will assure yourself that each point of contrast is discussed. If you are going to talk about the method of communication in physical discipline, then you will also talk about that in reasoning discipline.

In this paragraph, the writer has chosen to write about each idea separately. This method is called **one side at a time**. In this method, the writer will say everything about one of the topics and then everything about the other.

However, the organization within those discussions is very important. If the writer talks about physical discipline by first mentioning the type of 'communication' between parent and child, then when the writer begins his discussion of reasoning discipline, he must also discuss the type of 'communication' found between parent and child first.

The order of topics in the first part of the paragraph (the discussion of physical discipline) must match the order of topics in the second part of the paragraph (the discussion of reasoning discipline.) So even if the writer chooses to discuss each type of discipline separately, he must discuss the **same points about each one in the same order**.

1-2. Point by Point

> 위의 paragraph를 "point by point" 방식으로 contrast한 paragraph입니다.

Here is another way to organize the paragraph:

There are two different ways to discipline children – one promotes physical punishment and one that promotes reason. Physical punishment is practiced by some parents who believe that a little bit of discomfort will deter children from repeating an unacceptable action. Parents will slap a child's hand if he touches something forbidden, or pat a child's bottom if he behaves badly. On the other hand, some parents believe that reasoning with a child is the best method of discipline. They do not believe that a child should be hit at any time. Parents who believe in physical discipline state that a child, in a dangerous situation, will respond quickly to a sharp tap on the hand, bottom or leg. They feel that the instant reaction may actually keep a child safe. However, parents who feel that reasoning is the best method will talk to the child and get him to understand why his behavior is not appropriate. Thus, children learn to understand the reasons why parents are not pleased with them, and they will then stop before they do the same thing another time, and this thinking process will keep them safe from harm. In physical discipline, the danger of course is that the parent will forget his or her own strength and hit the child too hard. There is a fine line between physical discipline and abuse. In the 'reasoning' method, there is no danger that a child will be harmed physically as at no time will the parent impose his strength on the child, however, a child may not learn immediately and thus his behavior might be repeated. There are certainly advantages to both methods of discipline; however, recent studies seem to indicate that a child who is physically disciplined may mimic the parent and use similar tactics when dealing with others.

In this paragraph, instead of giving all the information about physical discipline and then all the information about reasoning discipline, the writer has compared them **point by point.** He first mentions that physical disciplinarians 'slap' children, and follows that by saying that parents who believe in reasoning with their children do not believe in hitting.

Both the point by point and one side at a time methods are acceptable in comparison and contrast paragraphs.

Point by Point is used more frequently in longer pieces of writing, since writing everything about one idea at the beginning of a long essay will mean that the reader is likely to forget it all by the end. The point by point method keeps both ideas present all the way through the writing.

What you have just learned about planning a **contrast** paragraph is true for a **comparison** paragraph as well.

2. Comparison Paragraph

> 두 사물의 서로 비슷한 점을 분석하는 Comparison Paragraph의 예문입니다.

Here is a **comparison** paragraph:

My mother and I have a tremendous number of things in common. First of all, we both look very much alike. I have always had very thick, dark brown hair and so has my mother. As well, I have piercing dark eyes and a very long nose just like her. In the pictures taken of my mother and me at similar ages, it is hard to distinguish who is who. Even our smiles are the same. As well, full figure pictures of us both as young women show only too well the similar tilt of our heads, our long legs, and the inward twist of our feet as we stand for a photo. Now as we are getting older and my mother's hair is starting to go grey, the physical similarities seem less but there are still so many traits that identify us as family. I have a silly little laugh that erupts at the strangest times, and so does my mother. Both our laughs start as giggles in our throats and end up as howls of pleasure. Our sense of humor is the same as well. We laugh at the same things, and although neither of us tell jokes very well, we love to listen to others tell them. But we are the same in anger as well as humor. When we are annoyed, the telltale wrinkles appear above our eyes and grow into deep furrows across our whole brow. Our dark eyes become steely grey and our lips become thin lines. We are lucky though, since anger is a rare occurrence for either one of us. It is strange to look into the mirror sometimes and think that perhaps you are looking at someone else, but then, it is comforting too to know that there is someone out there who is so much like you that they understand you as no one else ever can.

 Exercise 2

1) What does the writer say in the topic sentence to indicate that there will be a comparison in the paragraph?

2) In what three ways do the mother and the writer look alike?

3) Which pattern does the writer use – point by point or one side at a time?

3. Comparison-Contrast Paragraph

두 사물을 서로 비슷한 점과 서로 다른 점을 분석하는 Comparison-Contrast Paragraph의 예문입니다..

In the last lesson, we talked about paragraphs that either compared or contrasted. But sometimes you will be asked to write a paragraph that does both. Here is an example of a **comparison-contrast** paragraph.

    Although the elements found in Science Fiction and Fantasy writing are often similar, there are some distinct differences between the two styles. Both forms of writing contain elements of unreality; however, even in this element, there is disparity. Science Fiction, although imaginary, has, at its basis, a scientific possibility. That is to say, that even if the story contains ideas that, at the moment seem unbelievable, it is possible that they may become possible at some point in the future. But in Fantasy writing, there is no hope for that possibility. In Science Fiction, we may meet strange machines such as computers that can think. With all the technological advancements in our world, a talking computer is not beyond the realm of possibility. Fantasy, however, is filled with magic spells, talking dragons, dwarves, and fairies. These, no matter how delightful, are not within possibility in the real world. As well, Science Fiction and Fantasy share tales of the future and the past, great adventures which stimulate the reader's imagination. But their purposes in telling stories are very different. Fantasy is written as sheer entertainment whereas Science Fiction comes with a strong message to the reader.

Exercise 3

1) What is similar about Science Fiction and Fantasy?

2) How are the two types of writing different?

3) What transitional expressions in the paragraph emphasize similarities and differences?

Before writing this comparison-contrast paragraph, the writer probably brainstormed to gather ideas and then made a plan like this:

<u>Topic sentence:</u> *Although the elements found in Science Fiction and Fantasy writing are often similar, there are some distinct differences between the two styles.*

<u>Comparisons:</u> both use elements that are 'unreal
both appeal to the imagination of the reader
both tell tales of the future and the past

<u>Contrasts:</u> Science Fiction: based on science - believable
Fantasy: based in imagination – not believable

Science Fiction: uses things we know and relate to (talking computers for example)
Fantasy: uses magic, talking animals, unreal creatures

Science Fiction: has a message for the reader
Fantasy: no message, just entertainment

A plan such as this makes it easier for the writer to organize a great deal of material. The writer begins by listing all the points of comparison (how they are similar) and then he lists all the points of contrast (how they are different).

Transitions

> Comparison–Contrast Paragraph에 사용되는 Transition에 대해 공부합니다.

You have learned the importance of transitional expressions in paragraphs. Here are some that are particularly helpful in writing these types of paragraphs.

Transitional Expressions for Contrast
These transitional expressions stress opposition and difference:

Although	whereas	but	unlike	on the other hand
in contrast	yet	conversely	while	however

Transitional Expressions for Comparison
Transitional expressions in comparison paragraphs stress similarities:

| also | as well as | both | too | each of | in the same way |
| in addition | similarly | like | the same | and | just as ... so |

Be sure to use different transitional expressions in your writing. Don't just use a couple from the list! Try them all out at some time in your paragraphs!

 Exercise 4

Here are several topics for either contrast or comparison paragraphs. Compose two topic sentences for each topic, one for a possible contrast paragraph and one for a possible comparison paragraph.

> Example:
> *Topic:*   *Two friends of mine*
> *Topic Sentence for Contrast:*
>   *My two friends Angie and Toni have different ideas about diets.*
> *Topic Sentence for Comparison:*
>   *My two friends Bob and John are both very clever people.*

1) Topic: *Two countries*
   Topic Sentence for Contrast:

   Topic Sentence for Comparison

2) Topic: *Two movies*
   Topic Sentence for Contrast:

   Topic Sentence for Comparison

3) Topic: *Two vacations*
   Topic Sentence for Contrast:

   Topic Sentence for Comparison

4. Developing a Comparison or Contrast Essay

4-1. Choose Topic Wisely

> Comparison Contrast Essay를 쓰기 위해서는 서로 비슷한 점 또는 서로 다른 점이 있는, 즉 비교 가능한 두 사물을 선택하여야 합니다.

Be sure that there is a valid basis for comparing or contrasting the two ideas, people or items that you have chosen.

For example:
You could compare and contrast the television shows "Friends" and "Frasier". Both of these shows are situation comedies and it is possible to talk about the characters, the humor, and the themes of the shows.

But you really could not compare "Friends" and "Dr. Phil". One is a situation comedy and the other is a self-help/talk show. There is no common basis between the two.

4-2. Point of View.

> 두 사물에 대해 Comparison (비슷한 점)과 Contrast (서로 다른 점) 중에 어떤 관점으로 essay를 전개할 것인지 결정합니다.

Make sure that you have a point of view. When you have decided how you feel about each side of the issue, then you will be able to write your thesis statement. It will also help you in your choice of supporting details.

For example:
If you are listing the points that you would use to compare life in Canada to life in Korea, you may discover that there are good points to both countries. Gradually, your thesis will develop. It will state that both countries are great places to live, but in different ways.

Another example:
You have been asked to compare the poetry of Shakespeare and of Edgar Allen Poe. You list the points of similarity between the two and then the points of contrast. You decide that they are more different than they are similar, so your thesis may state: "Although Edgar Allen Poe and William Shakespeare are both highly regarded poets, their poetry is worlds apart." (worlds apart: 현격히 차이나다)

4-3. Limit the Topic

> 하나의 essay에 포함될 수 있는 내용으로 Topic의 범위를 좁힙니다.

Be sure that you limit the topic to a size that is manageable in a five-paragraph essay. If your topic is too large, you may end up stating only general observations.

Too broad:	American and Imported Cars
Better:	American cars do not perform as well as Japanese Cars.

4-4. Importance and Relevance

> Comparison Contrast Essay에서 비교할 수 있는 모든 점을 다 언급할 수는 없습니다. 중요하고 관련 있는 점만 언급합니다.

Make sure that all the points of comparison are important and relevant. You do not need to mention all the things that are the same or different. If you are comparing Nicole Kidman and Catherine Zeta-Jones, for example, there is no value in saying that they are both tall; once you've stated that, what more can be said on that subject? Points need to be significant.

4-5. Choose Method of Development

> One-side-at-a-time과 Point-by-point 방식 중 어느 방식으로 전개할 것인지 결정합니다.

As discussed before, there are two methods that can be used to develop your basis for comparison or contrast, **one-side-at-a-time** and **point-by-point**. It is important for you to decide which of the two methods you are going to use before you write your essay.

If you choose to use the point-by-point comparison, check to be sure that each of the points you develop is approximately the same length. If one paragraph is very long and the others are quite short, then you probably need to look at your topic and try to narrow it a bit further. In some cases, the longer point might make the topic of the whole essay.

4-6. Be Interesting

> 독자에게 새로운 정보를 줄 수 있는 흥미로운 Topic을 선정하여야 합니다.

Your topic needs to be interesting, but it must also be significant. Don't tell your audience what they already know. Choose a topic that might help the reader learn something. For example, a topic about the differences between high school and university is not really going to add to the reader's experience.

4-7. Analyze

> Comparison Contrast Essay의 목적은 analysis (분석)입니다. 분석 없이 단순히 비슷한 점, 틀린 점을 나열하는 것은 좋은 essay가 아닙니다.

Remember that the purpose of your essay is to analyze, not just to state the similarities and differences between two things/people/concepts.

Sample Essay #1 - One Side at a Time

Using this method of development, you state some point of comparison or contrast and then provide all the details to support that point – first for one side, and then for the other. Each paragraph will contain one point of comparison or contrast.

Read through the following essay on choosing between two vehicles, which illustrates the one-side-at-a-time method.

*To Everything There Is a Season (I)

I have always loved Corvettes (고급스포츠카), but now that I have children, a Corvette no longer meets my family's needs. It would not be easy to give up my "toy", but I have to think about a new vehicle – the dreaded minivan! Although a Corvette and a van both fulfill the basic requirement of transportation, I have to consider their differences in size, price and usability.

The disparate dimensions of the vehicles were the first consideration. Sitting in a minivan after the sports car was like sitting on a Clydesdale (말의 한종류) after riding a pony. I was amazed at the amount of room in the van and it was so easy to get in and out of the seats, even those in the back! However, when I dropped the pencil I was making notes with and it rolled under the minivan's back seat, I had to fumble around the floor of the vehicle and in the end, I couldn't find the pencil. Unlike the minivan, a Corvette sits almost on the ground. I have to do a lot of bending and stooping to get the baby's car seat into the car. And because the Corvette only has two seats, I am compelled to jam the groceries into a tiny space behind the front seats. But the Corvette is so small that it is easy to retrieve anything from under the seats.

There are also cost differences. First is the price of gasoline. The minivan would use the basic, non-premium gasoline. With the cost of fuel these days, the van would certainly save me some money. As well, the minivan would get very good mileage. The biggest cost difference would come with the initial price of the vehicle. The minivan is an average priced vehicle and I could afford to add some extras to it. Insurance costs were another consideration. The cost of insuring a van is reasonable, and because parts are readily available, the cost to fix the van after an accident is not exorbitant. Gas for the Corvette has been a major expense since I have been treating my Corvette with kid gloves, putting high octane gasoline in the tank. As well, the Corvette drinks gas like an alcoholic drinks beer. The original cost of a Corvette is higher than that of a van, and if you want to add extras, the price tag gets even higher. Plus, even though I am over twenty-five and have a clean driving record, I still pay significantly higher premiums to insure a sports car, and an accident in a Corvette involves major rebuilding because of the fiberglass body.
(treat~ with kid glove: ~을 신중히[부드럽게] 다루다)

The deciding factor of course is the usability of the two vehicles. The minivan has at least five seats, and often seven. With a growing family and a dog, the more seating, the better. As well, the children often like to bring their friends along on holidays and outings, so a minivan is the perfect answer. Car pooling is also possible with the minivan, and that will help to reduce fuel costs and our impact on the environment. The Corvette has only two seats, and although I love the idea of getting out on my own or with only one other person, the seating is a real problem in family life. The Corvette does not allow families to travel together, and, let's face it, when you have children, you really do travel with them most of the time.

Giving up my Corvette would hurt, there's no doubt about that; it has been my pride and joy for a long time. But I am a parent now, and must accept the responsibility for the care, comfort and safety of my children. Traveling with my family is a joy, and if it takes a minivan to make the journey a pleasant one, then a minivan it is!
* To Everything There Is a Season: 성경말씀, 천하만사가 다 때가 있나니.

Exercise 5

1) What three sentences does the writer use to indicate the three points of comparison that are explored in the essay? Underline them.

2) Which choice of vehicle does the writer discuss first in each body paragraph?

3) What five points of contrast does the writer use in the second body paragraph?

4) What is the writer's purpose in the concluding paragraph of the essay?

Sample Essay #2 – Side by Side

Below is the essentially same essay as the one you just read; however, this time the points are arranged side by side. That means that one point is made about the minivan, and then the same point is considered about the Corvette. As in the first method, the writer must state the point of comparison or contrast.

Read the essay again with this new arrangement.

To Everything There Is a Season (II)

     I have always loved Corvettes, but now that I have children, a Corvette no longer meets my family's needs. It would not be easy to give up my "toy", but I have to think about a new vehicle – the dreaded minivan! Although a Corvette and a van both fulfill the basic requirement of transportation, I have to consider the differences in size, price and usability.

     Sitting in a minivan after the sports car was like sitting on a Clydesdale after riding a pony. Unlike a Corvette, which is very low to the ground, the minivan was so high that I felt like a delivery truck driver. I was amazed at the amount of room in the van and it was so easy to get in and out of the seats, even those in the back. This was a tremendous contrast to the bending and stooping that I have to do to get the baby's car seat into the Corvette. And, of course, the Corvette doesn't have a back seat, so I have to jam the groceries into a tiny space behind the front seats. However, when I dropped the pencil I was making notes with and it rolled under the minivan's back seat, I had to fumble around the floor of the van and in the end, I couldn't find the pencil. That would never happen in the Corvette. The size of the vehicles is a major issue to consider.

     There are also cost differences. First is the price of gasoline. I had been treating my Corvette with kid gloves, putting high octane gasoline in the tank. But the minivan would use the basic, non-premium gasoline. With the cost of fuel these days, the van would certainly save me some money. As well, the Corvette drinks gas like an alcoholic drinks beer. Despite its greater size, the minivan would get better gas mileage. The biggest cost difference would come with the initial price of the vehicle. A Corvette is far more expensive than the van would be, even if I added several luxury extras to the basic minivan price tag. Insurance costs are yet another consideration. Although I am over twenty-five and have a clean driving record, the cost to insure a sports car is significantly more than the cost of insuring a van. And then there is also the cost to fix the two cars. An accident in a Corvette involves major surgery because of the fiberglass body. A similar accident in a minivan is far less expensive to fix.

The deciding factor of course is the usability of the two vehicles. The Corvette has only two seats, and although I love the idea of getting out on my own or with only one other person, the seating is a real problem in family life. The Corvette does not allow families to travel together, and, let's face it, when you have children, you really do travel with them most of the time. As well, the children often like to bring their friends along on holidays and outings, so a minivan is the perfect answer. The minivan allows everyone, even the family dog, to have a comfortable, roomy seat.

Giving up my Corvette would hurt, there's no doubt about that; it has been my pride and joy for a long time. But I am a parent now, and must accept responsibility for the care, comfort and safety of my children. Traveling with my family is a joy, and if it takes a minivan to make the journey a pleasant one, then a minivan it is!

 ## Exercise 6

1) Which paragraph in the essay has its topic sentence at the end of the paragraph rather than at the beginning?

2) The writer changes the order in which the vehicles are contrasted. Which body paragraph should be changed to follow the pattern established in the other two?

3) Name three transitions used in the second body paragraph.

✎ Writing Exercise

Write a five-paragraph essay of comparison or contrast on one of the topics below. Your essay must be 400-600 words in length.

- two schools you've attended
- two places you've visited
- two friends (or enemies) you have
- two kinds of music
- two types of food that you enjoy (or really don't like)
- two of your favorite books

Prewriting

1. Select your topic and remember that you are not going to **describe** the two things; you are going to **emphasize** the ways that they are alike or different. Students often fall into the problem of writing simple descriptions, and the essay does not accomplish its purpose.

2. Make two columns on a sheet of paper, one for each of the things that you are going to write about. In the first column, write down all the ideas that you can think of to describe the thing you are writing about. Then, in the second column, write down a corresponding word or phrase about the item in the other column.

For example:

Corvette	Minivan
- two seats	- five to seven seats
- costs a lot to buy	- mid-priced car
- costs a lot to insure	- insurance rates are average
- runs on high octane fuel	- runs on regular gasoline
- gets low mileage to the liter	- good mileage per liter
- no car pooling	- can carry kids, dogs, friends
- small interior	- big interior for groceries

When the writer of the essay looked at the list above, he realized that there were more differences between the two vehicles than similarities. So, the essay would **emphasize**

the differences (contrasts) between the Corvette and the minivan.

When the writer looked at the list, he also could see that the points fell into three basic categories: size, cost, and usability.

3. As you look over your lists, think how the characteristics you've written down could fit into three categories that will serve as your main points.

4. Decide how you will organize your essay. Be consistent with your choice of method and in the way you organize your paragraphs.

5. Complete the attached Essay Outline Sheet.

6. Write your essay.

ESSAY OUTLINE

Thesis:

Method of Introduction:

Method of Organization (circle one): Time Order, Emphatic Order, Space Order

Three Main Ideas
*First_____

<u>Examples/Illustrations/Supporting Details</u>
-
-
-

*Second_____

<u>Examples/Illustrations/Supporting Details</u>
-
-
-

*Third_____

<u>Examples/Illustrations/Supporting Details</u>
-
-
-

Method of Conclusion:

Answer Keys

Lesson 1
Exercise 1: 1) a: People should not drink and drive, b: 50% of all accidents are alcohol related, Alcohol reduces a person's reaction time, drunk drivers often fall asleep at the wheel, a drunk driver may not be able to see clearly,
2) a: Parents who read to their children on a regular basis are doing their children a great favor, b: Children develop a life long love of reading, Children are better readers if they have been read to as infants, Children who read are better writers, Children who are read to develop a strong sense of language,
3) a: There are a lot of things to consider when choosing the best university to attend, b: location, strong academic environment, good sports/leisure program, good reputation with employers
Exercise 2: 1) d, 2) c, 3) c
Exercise 3: Answers will vary. Suggestions only 1) At all stages of life, people have access to injections that will help them stay healthy. 2) Cats are better pets than dogs.

Lesson 2
Exercise 1: 1) Topic: My best friend, Controlling Idea: the funniest person I know, 2) Topic: skating in the winter, Controlling Idea: I love it, 3) Topic: music, Controlling Idea: makes life enjoyable, 4) Topic: Working with animals, Controlling Idea: rewarding experience, 5) Topic: The movie "Kong", Controlling Idea: outstanding special effects
Exercise 2: Answers will vary.

Lesson 3
Exercise 1: Answers will vary.
Exercise 2: 1) 1, 3, 5 2) 1, 3, 4
Exercise 3: 1) Some trucks have two kinds of horns. The police sirens have changed in the last few years. And most cities have lots of malls for people to visit! 2) Many children would like to be able to do magic. But kids should not think that Harry Potter is real! Sometimes a child will need to ask a parent for the meaning of a word in the novel. 3) Hair styles and jewelry might become focal points for competitiveness among girls, but schools can impose rules to restrict hair fashion and accessories. It is important to encourage creativity.

Lesson 4

Exercise 1: next, then, after, finally

Exercise 2: 1) 2, 3, 5, 4, 1 2) 2, 3, 5, 1, 4, 6 3) 2, 4, 3, 1 4) 2, 1, 4, 3

Exercise 3: 1) Honesty is one of the greatest virtues in society, 2) Honesty allows people to deal with themselves and others on a clear footing, without pretense, 3) But most importantly, 4) Honesty keeps the lines of communication open, 5) More importantly, 6) Being honest is good for the soul.

Exercise 4: 1) When the tsunami of December 2004 hit the coast of Indonesia, the results were horrific. 2) Over 300,000 lives were lost in the destruction, 3) at the beginning, 4) another result of the tsunami was economic, 5) the last point in the paragraph

Lesson 6

Exercise 1: Answers will vary.

Exercise 2: 1) b, 2) c, 3) a, 4) b, 5) a

Lesson 7

Exercise 1: **Answers will vary. Sample answers only** 1) Slowly Sandra walked all the way downtown 2) To win the game, the boys tried to play their best at all times 3) During the basketball game, the referee made several bad calls. 4) Crowded with Christmas shoppers, the stores in the mall were noisy and hot. 5) Fishing for only an hour, Bob managed to catch five large fish.

Exercise 2: **Answers will vary. Sample answers only** 1) Semi-colon: I love to grow things; I have a big garden every summer, Adverb: I love to grow things; therefore, I have a big garden every summer, 2) Semi-colon: Mona is not feeling well; she is sleeping a lot during the day, Adverb: Mona is not feeling well; therefore, she is sleeping a lot during the day, 3) Semi-colon: My brother had a car accident last week; he is going to buy a new vehicle soon, Adverb: My brother had a car accident last week; consequently, he is going to buy a new vehicle soon, 4) Semi-colon: Our cat ran away last week; she came back this morning, Adverb: Our cat ran away last week; however, she came back this morning, 5) Semi-colon: The aircraft that we were riding in had very hard seats; we were very uncomfortable for the whole trip, Adverb: The aircraft that we were riding in had very hard seats; consequently, we were very uncomfortable for the whole trip.

Exercise 3: 1) Our class includes the following successful people: John Dean, president of Yale University; Anne Fortune, chairperson of Auto Canada; and Virginia Dole, Minister of Finance for Alberta. 2) The Art Gallery of Scotch Creek is pleased to display the following paintings: 'Echo', by John O'Toole; 'Treescape', by Marion McVeen; 'Foolishness', by Andrew Carter; and 'England', by Annette Andrews.

Exercise 4: 1) Jim and John are going to California this week; however, they are not going to Disneyland. 2) I have a very sore throat; I am going to see the doctor this afternoon. 3)

Ginny is not going to the party tonight; instead, she is staying home to look after her little sister. 4) I want to learn to write well; consequently, I must learn grammar. 5) I am very hungry; I am going to make something to eat.

Exercise 5: **Answers will vary. Sample answers only** 1) The dog wouldn't come when it was called so the owner put him on a leash. 2) My friend went looking for a job yesterday and found one at the local supermarket 3) Our cat really enjoys being outdoors but she likes to sit by the fireplace in the evening 4) My father really loves to read but he has read so many books that it is difficult to find one that he hasn't read.

Exercise 6: **Answers will vary. Sample answers only** 1) I went to the dentist because I had a toothache OR Because I had a toothache, I went to the dentist 2) When the man sat down on the chair, it broke. OR The chair broke when the man sat down on it. 3) After our car broke down for the third time, we decided to buy a new one. OR We decided to buy a new car after our old one broke down for the third time.

Exercise 7: **Answers will vary. Sample answers only** 1) The dog ran out of the yard, down the street, and into the store 2) The noisy, crowded cafeteria served greasy, cold food. 3) By midnight I had finished my essay, edited it carefully, typed it up on the computer and printed it out to hand in the next day. 4) The fat old bear sat on the rotten log. 5) The young, inexperienced doctor took the miserable old patient's temperature.

Exercise 8: **Answers will vary. Sample answers only** 1) Combining #1: Television reality shows are very popular today; they deal with so called real life situations. Combining #2: Television reality shows deal with so called real life situations that are very popular today. 2) Combining #1: Rock and Roll developed in the 1950's and 1960's with one of the earliest stars being Elvis Presley; also, Buddy Holly made Rock and Roll popular with the teens of that age. Combining #2: Elvis Presley and Buddy Holly made Rock and Roll very popular with the teens during the 1950's and 1960's. 3) Combining #1: People who were born in the 1920's have seen an amazing number of advancements including the telephone, the television, the car, and the computer which are all major technological advances in the past one hundred years. Combining #2: People who were born in the 1920's have seen an amazing number of inventions in the past one hundred years; these inventions include the telephone, the television, the car and the computer. 4) Combining #1: Jean is a really good student who does especially well in English and Science. Combining #2: Jean does especially well in English and Science; he is a really good student.

Exercise 9: **Answers will vary. Sample answers only** 1) My name is Sam and I am an immigrant from France. Since I can't speak English, and most of my friends can't speak French, I am finding it hard to adapt to my new country. I miss my friends from my hometown near Paris, however, I like Canada and I want to learn to be happy here. 2) At Christmas, we have lots of traditional foods. Since we have turkey, dressing, vegetables, potatoes, apple and mince pie as well as shortbread, we always eat too much. 3) I love rainy days if they don't come too often. When it rains, I stay inside and find a lot of interesting things to do. I watch my favorite television programs, read books, play computer games, and have a nap whenever I want. Although sunny days are great, there is something nice about the sound of a gentle rain.

Lesson 8

Exercise 1: **Answers will vary. Sample answers only** 1) We had a relaxing vacation in Paris. 2) The girl in the commercial was very attractive. 3) The woman had a very wrinkly and haggard looking face. 4) Every morning I wake up and look into the mirror my face looks pale and tired. 5) I read a thrilling book last week. 6) The coffee that she made tasted awful. The coffee that he made was not delicious. 7) We had a memorable experience at the zoo. 8) What a nurturing and comical father he is!

Exercise 2: **Answers will vary. Sample answers only** 1) The girls were gossiping at the lunch table. The girls were whispering at the lunch table. 2) The boys chuckled when the teacher walked by their desk. The boys howled with laughter when the teacher walked by their desk. 3) The dog dived into the water. The dog jetted into the water. 4) I witnessed the accident and I reported it to the police. I viewed the accident and I reported it to the police.

Exercise 3: 1) Careful campers remember to put out their fires, to leave he campsite clean, and to remove all their garbage. 2) The waiter at the restaurant reminded us that we should order quickly, eat slowly and tip well. 3) You will be responsible for planning the party, buying the food, and cleaning the room 4) The hardware store sells hand tools, home appliances and building materials 5) In order to become an actress, Anne is taking drama lessons, working for a theatre company, and auditioning for roles. 6) At the beauty salon, I had my hair washed, dried, and colored. 7) Many people like to go on vacation, to spend money, and to sleep late in the morning. 8) To be a good role model you should consider your behavior, your relationships with others and your appearance in public, 9) Modern appliances will help you to do the laundry, cook food and wash dirty dishes. 10) Mike likes movies that are suspenseful, interesting and exciting.

Lesson 9

Exercise 1: 1) I used to love watching television. I turned the TV on after dinner each night and settled in for an evening of great entertainment. Crime shows, game shows, reality shows, I knew them all! 2) Watching television these days is a waste of time. 3) a. there are so many interruptions in programs, b. shows are unoriginal, c. there far too many repeats in programs, 4) To begin with, I just don't like the constant interruptions for commercials, 5) a. too many ads in one show b. too many ads at the same time c. too many repetitions of ads, 6) As well as endless advertising, I am finding that television shows lack any originality. 7) a. Survivor-type shows, b. Crime –type shows, c. 'Idol'-type shows, 8) It isn't just the commercials, or the sameness of the shows that drive me crazy, it is also the fact that there are too many repetitions of shows. 9) a. not enough new episodes for a full season, b. repetitions of old shows throughout the season, c. shows replayed several times on the same channel in a single day, 10) It really is a waste of time to turn on the television these days 11) Getting through a ton of commercials only to watch a boring reality show or a rerun, just isn't worth the effort.

Lesson 10

Exercise 1: 2, 4, 7, 8, 11, 13, 14, 18, 19, 20

Exercise 2: Answers will vary. Sample answers only 1) Police should have greater authority in punishing people who speed. (needs to be more concise, specific ideas can be expressed in the body paragraphs), 2) The profession of a plumber and electrician have many similarities. OR The profession of a plumber and electrician are very different (must pick one side of the argument to show unity), 3) Skiing is a very dangerous winter sport.(needs to express an opinion), 4) Vancouver is one of the most expensive Canadian cities. (needs a focus, not just a fact), 5) Buying a house is a very large investment which requires a considerable amount of preparation.

Exercise 3: Answers will vary.

Exercise 4: **Answers will vary. Sample answers only** 1) My choice of vehicle has always been a sign of my stage in life. 2) A person should choose a post secondary institution to match his vocation goals. 3) Losing weight for me has been a losing battle. 4) Christmas is the best holiday of the year.

Exercise 5: Answers will vary.

Exercise 6: Answers will vary.

Exercise 7: Answers will vary.

Exercise 8: 1) All parents enjoy the process of raising their children. Although there are both good times and difficult moments, watching children grow and develop is exciting and rewarding. While there is much to be said for parenthood, there is another stage of raising children that is even better. 2) Being a grandparent is one of the greatest joys in a person's life. 3) Grandparents can take their grandchildren to special places, tell them wonderful stories, and best of all, spoil them completely. 4) Taking grandchildren out for a day is a treat for both the children and the grandparents. 5) Grandparents are very patient people and they have lots of time to read to their grandchildren 6) The best part of being a grandparent is that you can spoil your grandchildren

Lesson 11

Exercise 1: Answers will vary.

Exercise 2: 1) question, 2) mirror, 3) call for action

Lesson 12

Exercise 1: 1) first of all, next, in addition, finally, 2) first, next, before, while, finally, 3) next to, to the left, on the right, on the opposite side, near, 4) however, still, yet, but, 5) for example, such as, for instance, 6) consequently, as a result

Exercise 2: 1) patience, self discipline, self-discipline, kindness to others, 2) rising insurance costs, gasoline prices, high insurance costs, maintenance, 3) breathe clean air, clean air, free from the noise of traffic and people, slower pace

Exercise 3: **Answers will vary. Sample answers only** 1) In addition to listening to music, I like to do yoga to relax, 2) As well as doing yoga, tai chi and meditation, I often exercise to get rid of stress.

Exercise 4: 1) First of all, Then, Another, However, 2) Second, Then, As a result, On the contrary, After, 3) Last of all, In addition, But

Lesson 13

Exercise 1: Answers will vary.

Exercise 2: 1) facts, 2) the facts come from a reliable source, 3) raised crime rate, raised severity of crime, bankruptcies, availability of lottery tickets, increases in sales of tickets, 4) Although the Canadian government makes a great deal of money from the various gambling venues, it must consider the cost in human terms.

Exercise 3: 1) Not a valid source. Tobacco companies want your business so they will say anything to get you to buy the product, 2) Not a valid source. The source is biased. The local dealer wants your money, so they will say what they need to get your business, 3) isolated incident, 4) isolated incident, 5) exaggerated consequence, 6) insulting to the opposition, 7) isolated incident, 8) exaggerated consequence, 9) insulting the opposition

Lesson 14

Exercise 1: 1) The second body paragraph. 2) Other sports, such as American football or rugby, are also barely-concealed violence. 3) In the same way, 4) it acknowledges the opposition's point of view, 5) also, 6) at the end of the paragraph, 7) Moreover, sport teaches and requires discipline, training, and respect for the rules - valuable lessons in any society. 8) Nobody denies that regulation is needed. 9) call for action, 10) in conclusion

Exercise 2: Answers will vary.

Exercise 3: 1) However, despite the confined habitat of the zoo, the animal is better off than it would be in the wilds. 2) In captivity, there are no predators, diseases are dealt with, and food is always available. 3) Some people feel that imprisonment of animals in these confined areas is cruel punishment, and that zoos should be abolished in favor of allowing the animals to roam in their own environment. 4) However, 5) a) first of all, b) another, c) finally, 6) lower level animals in food chain, larger animals, and victims of the cat family, 7) mirror ending, 8) The zookeepers are trained to exercise the animals so that they stay healthy.

Lesson 15

Exercise 1: 1) four: child is not afraid of words, child is familiar with sounds of words and correct sentences, child gets ahead start in reading, child and parent spend time together, 2) recent studies in North America, 3) first of all, however, as well, finally

Exercise 2: 1) Cause: approaching tornado, Effect: ran down into the cellar, 2) Cause: laughter, Effect: can help cure disease, 3) Cause: severe injuries, Effect: schools ban football, 4) Cause: DVD use, Effect: movie theatre attendance decline, 5) Cause: dedication and hard work, Effect: great players

Exercise 3: 1) Women used to visit their neighbors for coffee in the mornings. 2) The modern world has brought new problems for marriages, 3) 1. The role of women in society has changed 2. There is greater stress in at home and in the workplace 3. Communication has become a thing of the past, 4) the causes, 5) another, as a result, 6) people don't communicate because: a. they are too busy with their jobs, b. they are too busy with their technologies

Exercise 4: Answers will vary.

Lesson 16

Exercise 1: 1)(funnel – general to specific, 2) it offers a final definition of the word "hero", 3) a) negation, b) negation, 4) origins, 5) examples

Exercise 2: 1) quotation, 2) what love is, what love is not, different types of love, 3) a) example, b) negation, 4) However, there are dangers that exist in the closeness of 'love', 5) five

Lesson 17

Exercise 1: Answers will vary.

Exercise 2: 1) However, therapy does not always deal with injured or mentally troubled people, 2) however, 3) physical, occupational, and speech therapies, 4) The writer has used the last sentence of the first category to introduce the next category in the essay. "But physical therapy is not the only type of therapy that involves the rehabilitation of injuries", 5) the first paragraph describes what Physical Therapy does. The second paragraph gives some background about Physical Therapy., 6) other, 7) The first paragraph describes what Occupational therapy does. The second paragraph talks about the writer's experience with Occupational therapy and then describes where OT happens and what qualifications are required to be an occupational therapist, 8) The writer refers back to the first and second categories to introduce the third category. "As well as physical and occupational therapy, speech therapy is another type of treatment that addresses some disabilities and injuries", 9) The writer repeats the categories. She also makes a prediction.

Lesson 18

Exercise 1: 1) two type of discipline – physical and reason, 2) child reacts quickly and in dangerous situations this reaction might keep the child safe, 3) danger that parent might hit too hard, 4) physical, 5) physical discipline can lead to inappropriate behavior on the part of children who mimic their parents, 6) answers will vary, but the focus should be on the fact that one type is discussed and then the second type is discussed separately, 7) on the other hand

Exercise 2: 1) number of things in common, 2) thick dark hair, piercing dark eyes, long noses, 3) point by point

Exercise 3: 1) both contain elements of unreality, both stimulate the imagination with tales of past and future, 2) Science Fiction has a basis in technology and science whereas Fantasy is simply imaginative. Science Fiction has a message, Fantasy does not, 3) but, however, as well…

Exercise 4: **Answers will vary. Sample answers only** 1) Topic Sentence for Contrast: Canada and the United States differ economically. Topic Sentence for Comparison: Canada and the United States both have democratic voting systems, 2) Topic Sentence for Contrast: Spiderman is an action movie, but The Notebook is a romance movie. Topic Sentence for Comparison: Spiderman and Batman are both use a lot of special effects, 3) Topic Sentence for Contrast: A vacation in a hotel is different than a vacation where you stay with relatives. Topic Sentence for Comparison: Mexico and Cuba both have all inclusive resorts.

Exercise 5: 1) The size of the vehicles was the first consideration. There were also cost differences. The deciding factor of course is the usability of the two vehicles, 2) the minivan, 3) cost of gasoline, gas mileage, original cost of the vehicle, cost of insurance, cost of repairs, 4) the writer shows that a decision has been made

Exercise 6: 1) body paragraph #1, 2) body paragraph #1, 3) first, as well, also

Essence Essay Writing

지은이 | 밴쿠버 SM Education

펴낸곳 | 마인드큐브
발행인 | 이상용
책임편집 | 홍원규
디자인 | 서용석

출판등록 | 제2018-000063호
이메일 | eclio21@naver.com
전   화 | 031-945-8046
팩   스 | 031-945-8047

초판 1쇄 발행 | 2012년 6월 15일
개정판 4쇄 발행 | 2024년 10월 21일

ISBN | 979-11-953277-3-7 13740

※ 잘못 만들어진 책은 바꾸어드립니다.
※ 이 책은 저작권법에 따라 보호받는 저작물이므로 무단전재와 무단복제를 금합니다.
※ 이 책의 일부 또는 전부를 이용하려면 반드시 저자와 마인드큐브의 동의를 받아야 합니다.